Published by **SAGAX** Publishing

Hereford Road

Monmouth, NP25 3GD, UK

Copyright © Keith Foster – April 2013

2nd Edition - Revised May 2015

ISBN 978-0-9532407-7-7

A catalogue record for this book is available from the British Library

Keith Foster's right to be identified as the author of this work has been asserted by him in accordance with the Copyright, Designs and Patents Act of 1988.

Manufacture / Printing coordinated in the UK by

LightningSource.com

All rights reserved. No part of this book may be reproduced or transmitted in any form, electronic or mechanical, including photocopy or any information storage and retrieval system, with permission in writing from the publisher.

HARMONIC POWER

PART II

GAIN

A WORD TO THE WISE

This book is written for informational and educational purposes only.

It is not intended to be used as medical advice.

©Keith Foster, April 2013

GAIN

CONTENTS

Page Number

- 3   The Beginning of Life on Earth
- 4   Iodine
- 12   The Salts of the Earth
- 18   Vitamin C
- 26   Oxygen
- 51   Cholesterol
- 54   Return to the Sea
- 60   Water
- 67   Chlorinated Water
- 71   Charcoal
- 78 C_{60} Charcoal & Longevity
- 87   Cooking

THE BEGINNING OF LIFE ON EARTH.

Two billion years ago a species of cyanobacteria evolved which covered the earth and changed the atmosphere.

These cyanobacteria, which are a bit like the spirolina you can buy in health food stores today, release a lot of free oxygen. Back then this free oxygen killed all organisms except those that developed a mechanism to deal with oxygen poisoning.

Oxygen, although it's vital to life as we know it, is poisonous.

This is because the use of oxygen creates highly reactive toxic bi-products called superoxides or free radicals which can damage any part of the body, including the immune system.

These are destroyed, or I should say, "mopped-up" in the body by enzyme complexes called superoxide dismutases (SODS). Dr. Richard Cutler of the National Institute on Ageing has shown that the SOD level in primates is highly correlated with longevity.

Fortunately, we don't have to rely solely on SODS because during our evolution our bodies also developed mechanisms to use the nutrient anti-oxidants Vitamin C, E and Selenium as very effective free radical controllers.

These offer protection against levels of radiation that would otherwise kill us in about 72 hours!

IODINE.

Iodine has an important and little understood history. This scarce element has played a pivotal role in the formation of our planet's atmosphere and the evolution of life.

For more than 2 billion years, as we've seen, there was no oxygen in the atmosphere until a new kind of bacteria, cyanobacteria (blue-green algae), began producing oxygen as a bi-product of photo synthesis. Cyanobacteria also developed an affinity for iodine!

The most likely reason is that these organisms used iodine as an anti-oxidant to protect themselves against free radicals (superoxide anion, hydrogen peroxide and hydroxyl radical) that oxygen breeds.

Studying kelp, researchers have shown how iodine does this and have found that kelp will absorb increased amounts of iodine when placed under oxidative stress. Other researchers have shown that iodine increases the anti-oxidant status of human serum similar to that of Vitamin C.

Iodine also induces apoptosis, programme cell death. This process is essential to growth and development since fingers form in the foetus by apoptosis of the tissue between them. It's also vital for destroying cells that represent a threat to the integrity of the organism, like cancer cells and cells infected with viruses.

Russian researchers first showed in 1966 that iodine effectively relieves signs and symptoms of fibrocystic breast disease.

Vishniakova and Murav'eva treated 167 women suffering from fibrocystic disease with 50 milligrams of potassium iodide during the inter-menstrual period and obtained the beneficial healing effect in 71%.

Then Ghent and co-workers in a study published in the Canadian Journal of Surgery in 1993 likewise found that iodine relieves signs and symptoms of fibrocystic breast disease in 70% of their patients.

A further study in Seattle which was statistically analysed, showed that iodine has a highly statistically significant beneficial effect on fibrocystic disease.

The FDA regard iodine as a natural substance not a drug and most physicians and surgeons view iodine from a narrow perspective (an antiseptic that disinfects drinking water and prevents surgical wounds infection and one needed by the thyroid to make thyroid hormones).

The thyroid gland needs iodine to synthesise hormones that regulate metabolism and steer growth and development and whilst the thyroid only needs trace amounts of iodine, there is a vast body of evidence that higher doses of iodine (above the RDA of 100 to 150 micrograms a day) will prevent a whole spectrum of disorders which would otherwise occur in its absence. According to English Professor Albert Guerard (1914 to 2000) the rest of the body also needs iodine in milligram amounts.

The Nobel Laureate Dr. Albert Szent-Györgyi (1893 to 1986) the physician who discovered Vitamin C, wrote: "When I was a medical student, iodine in the form of KI was the universal medicine. Nobody knew what it did, but it did something and did something good. We students used to sum up the situation in this little rhyme:-"

"If you don't know where, what and why, prescribe Ye then K and I."

The standard dose of potassium iodide given was 1 gram which contains 770 milligram of iodine.

Dr. Guy Abraham, a former professor of obstetrics and gynaecology at UCLA, mounted what he calls the iodine project in 1997 after he read the Ghent paper on iodine for fibrocystic disease.

The project's hypothesis is that maintaining whole-body sufficiency of iodine requires 12.5 milligram a day. An amount similar to what the Japanese consume! The project found that the vast majority of people retain a substantial amount of the 15 milligram dose and many require 50 milligram a day for several months before they will excrete 90% of it. His studies indicate that given a sufficient amount, the body will retain much more iodine than originally thought – 1,500 milligram, with only 3% of that amount being held in the thyroid gland.

More than 4,000 patients in this project take iodine in daily doses ranging from 12.5 to 50 milligram and those with diabetes take up to 100 milligram a day.

Thyroid function remains unchanged in 99% of patients and iodine removes the toxic halogens, fluoride and bromide, from the body.

To be fully healthy, we should emulate the Japanese and substantially increase our iodine intake, if not with seaweed, then with 2 drops of lugol's solution or one iodoral tablet a day.

To conclude, nowadays iodised table salt is a chief source of iodine in western diet but the bulk of people now buy salt without iodine, i.e. "table salt" which has all the trace elements driven off. Accordingly, over the last three decades, people who use iodised table salt have decreased their consumption by 65%, moreover, higher concentrations of chloride in salt (NaCl) inhibit absorption of its sister halogen, iodine.

Since the intestines only absorb 10% of the iodine present in iodised table salt, in order to stay healthy then it is vital to increase one's intake of iodine. You will find that everything in your body functions better, even your brain, once it's nourished by the iodine it needs. Without it you can't reach your full potential. The key here is to think of iodine not as a remedy but as a nutrient that is crucial to all aspects of health.

Your doctor will probably insist that you get all the iodine you need from fish and maybe you could if you consume 9 kilograms (20 1bs of fish a day and also withstand the mercury, PCB's and etc. now present in all fish).

2 drops of Lugol's per day in a glass of water is safe, an extremely conservative dose. Sometimes much higher amounts are necessary in the beginning to undo damage from years of deprivation.

Iodine supplementation brings about almost immediate lifting of spirits in mildly depressed people and does wonders to alleviate crankiness, which can go a long way toward preserving relationships! It also helps to banish long-established migraines.

Finally, because iodine in the cells prevents the uptake of radio active iodine (a different substance) then iodine is extremely effective as a preventative for mild radiation poisoning such as we are all susceptible to with the increase in background radiation due to atomic testing and atomic reactor disasters.

So as our distant ancestors, the cyanobacteria and, later on, the kelp discovered, iodine in sensible doses is an essential nutrient upon which good health depends.

So we've established why iodine is good for you in a general sort of way and more to the point how it helps prevent cancer. But we'll move on now to show how it can lengthen your life.

Currently our exposure to toxicalites, fluoride, bromide, petrochlorate and cyo cyanate (from cigarette smoke), is higher than humans have ever been exposed to in the past. Fluoride which is a strong neuro-toxin is added to drinking water supposedly to stop tooth decay and fluoride also gets into our systems when we ingest fluoride from sources such as pesticides, medicines, food, salt, toothpaste and health supplements.

Actually, fluoride fails to reduce tooth decay and there's quite a strong movement afoot to ban its use. However, that doesn't concern us so much as its very existence in our environment which contributes to early death.

Similarly, bromide. This toxic halide is everywhere. It's got an anti-bacterial function similar to chlorine and it's used as fumigant for agriculture and termites, it's a virulent pesticide that kills insects from contact and when it's injected into the soil everything dies. Because it's cheap and abundant, it appears in a vast number of food stuffs and has replaced iodine as a dough conditioner and is used widely in the milk industry because of its effective bactericide properties.

Iodine helps the body eliminate fluoride, bromine, lead, cadmium, arsenic, aluminium and mercury, so that when iodine was replaced by bromine in bread and milk etc. there was no longer a way to eliminate the bromine.

Overnight a huge segment of the population was being affected by bromine, since bread – "the stuff of life" - strikes us all.

In the 1920s a hugely popular hangover cure called bromo-seltzer worked so well that every medicine cabinet had one. The bad news about bromo-seltzer took about half a century to become common knowledge – too much of this hangover cure led to what became known as bromomania, details of which were published in the *New England Journal of Medicine*. And this shows that between 1920 and 1960 alarming numbers of bromo-seltzer victims landed in psychiatric hospitals with acute paranoid psychosis.

More recently during the Gulf war, the US government dosed personnel with pyridostigmine bromide to prevent death in the event of exposure to chemical warfare. As it happened chemical warfare didn't occur, but Gulf war syndrome did and it's almost impossible to locate the statistics on the number of service men and women who were sent home as incurably ill, hopeless psychotics.

The ubiquitous nature of bromide in food stuffs, particularly sodas, gives rise to morbid obesity. This is because when oil is placed in a bowl and bromine is stirred in, the bromine will slowly turn the liquid oil into a solid until it becomes so stiff that the spoon won't move. This happens once the bromine/oil mixture is in the body and this goes a long way to explaining the cause of our epidemic of obesity. As one Dr. Flechas pointed out, "years of drinking sodas that are loaded with brominated vegetable oil solidifies body fat.

Even more sinister are the words from Guy E. Abraham MD who claims that removal of iodine caused more misery and death than both world wars combined!

Iodine in sensible doses will both help the body release toxins and prevent the uptake of an abundance of pollution products, i.e. mercury from amalgam fillings, lethal artificial sweeteners, sodium fluoride and pesticide exposure, food additives, electromagnetic-radiation exposure, vaccinations, shocking agricultural practices, chemtrails, sugar, alcohol and severe toxicity caused by dependence on drugs.

Whilst iodine is not the universal panacea that it would appear from what I've just said, it is nevertheless a vital pivotal and fundamental part of any programme designed to both improve the quality and increase the length of one's life.

Adequate iodine levels are necessary for proper immune system function. Iodine contains potent anti-bacterial, anti-parasitic, anti-viral, and anti-cancer properties. Approximately 1.5 billion people (about one third of the earth's population) live in an area of iodine deficiency as defined by the World Health Organisation. Iodine-deficiency disorder is the most common preventable form of mental retardation known.

Iodine is responsible for the production of all the hormones of the body and oddly enough 20% of the body's store of iodine is in the skin! This is not entirely surprising in the context of an aquatic life form subject to high levels of radiation on leaving the water i.e. us and, as we shall see later, this aquatic lifestyle was not only the origin of our species, (indeed all species) but is one to which we have returned periodically during our long evolution.

THE SALTS OF THE EARTH.

Three billion years ago when the earth was still hot and covered by an atmosphere thick with dust and smoke, water formed in the atmosphere and rocks and it started to rain. Over millions of years the rain dissolved chemicals from the dust and gases in the atmosphere and since this rain was highly acidic, it also dissolved mineral salts and trace elements from the rocks and the soil.

Ultimately, these were transported down streams and rivers into the sea where they accumulated to form salt water. This salt water contained every mineral and trace element that was available in the earth's crust and atmosphere at that time and to this day the seas contain at least 85 different mineral salts and trace elements. These chemicals combined and recombined to form a vast array of chemical combinations, ultimately combining to form the basic building blocks of life on earth.

All of these are essential to life and we have recently established that every nutrient and essential element operates by multiple interactions in the human body. (I shall return to this in the next paper).

Prior to the appearance of cyanobacteria and the oxygen they produced, the only way energy could be produced in the chemical soup of our seas was by fermentation. Slowly, as our early large-celled protein ancestors developed, there was very little energy available to them, particularly as they only had fermentation to draw on and were made of relatively large clumsy macromolecules in which the electrons were held firmly in their orbits and have no mobility.

Electrons are the small negatively-charged particles that surround the atomic core of a molecule. To have a flow of energy, these have to move from molecule to molecule. This is called electron transport.

The only electron conductor/acceptor available to early dark life was a weak chemical mixture called methyl-glyoxal. This couldn't conduct energy very well but when attached to the proteins, it was a start and dark life/fermentation quickly cashed in on this advantage by beginning to form proper cells with cell walls and nuclei.

This is essentially the first step on life's ladder and one which I shall return to in the next paper on Vitamin C.

Blood.

It will come as no surprise since we originated, as did all life, in the sea, to learn that our blood has more or less the same mineral profile that the sea had in the Cambrian era about 2 billion years ago. The same applies to all life which began in the sea.

This primeval sea is the perfect electrolyte, very able to transport electrons through the metabolic pathways of our body, and is the essential conductor of life.

Without salt in our diet we cannot live, since without it there can be no intercellular communication and our bodies begin to fall apart.

We still maintain a profound relationship with the sea and salt but the salt I'm talking about is the salt formed by the evaporation of the sea or from ancient deposits in salt mines.

Until the Industrial Revolution, all of the salt we used came from the sea or from salt mines which are basically deposits of salt laid down millions of years ago. Unfortunately, we can't now safely use sea salt because a lot of research has shown that it has become ever more polluted with such dangerous substances as mercury, DDT, PCB, PAH's, dioxins and etc. (source: *Killer Fish* by Brian R. Clement PhD. ISBN 978-1-57067-285-9).

Moreover, the use of mine salt from earth deposits is also of questionable value since most of it is transformed into "table salt". "Table salt" is salt which has been dried to 12,000 degrees Fahrenheit to achieve a concentration of 97.5% of sodium chloride to which is then added chemicals like moisture absorbents and iodine. These additives are used to make it stay dry and pour more easily.

Unfortunately, this process drives off all of the trace elements which are vital to our full good health leaving behind substances (pure sodium chloride) which, if eaten in quantity, will dehydrate your cells and kill you.

Much has been written by dietary experts and government departments about the dangers of excess "table salt" consumption and moves are afoot presently in the UK to try and get the producers of processed foods to limit its use.

The problem is that the average consumption of "table salt" (i.e. pure sodium chloride) is 12 to 20 grams daily and yet our kidneys can only excrete between 5 and 7 grams a day. The rest is "parked" in our tissues where it causes localised dehydration and premature ageing. These factors contribute significantly to osteo and rheumatoid arthritis plus a whole host of other unwanted side-effects.

The spectrum of minerals and trace elements which existed in the sea at the time our blood gained its unique signature, is now very difficult to come by. In the past this spectrum of trace elements was supplied in abundance, not only by the complex salts from a healthy sea, but also by crops grown on healthy fertile land.

The alarming fact nowadays is that foods (fruit, vegetables and grains) are now being raised on millions of acres of land that no longer contains enough of certain minerals. No matter how much of them we eat, our body is not getting enough of the needed spectrum of trace elements and we are starving! This problem was recognised as far back as 1936 in document 264 issued by the United States Senate, and I quote:-

"Our physical well being is far more directly dependent upon the minerals we take into our system than upon calories or vitamins or upon precise portions of starch, protein or carbohydrates we consume…do you know that most of us today are suffering from certain dangerous dietary deficiencies which cannot be remedied until depleted soils from which our food comes are brought into proper mineral balance!"

That was in 1936 and with the boom in NPK fertilisers and other modern farming methods, the situation has got worse.

To return to full good health, you need the minerals and trace elements which are missing from your diet and there are only two ways to get them. The first way is to grow your own food using only natural fertilisers and no chemical additives. (No pesticides, fungicides, herbicides or any of the other 17 or 18 sprayings that crops these days are subjected to).

The second way is to supplement your diet with very ancient sea salt shown to have a similar mineral and trace element profile to the seas we came from!

Salt deposits differ around the world just as mineral and trace element constituents of healthy soil differ. So it's important to appraise the health of the human and animal populations living in regions of the world where various salt deposits occur, in order to secure the supply of only those salts which support the most healthy populations.

I have identified and analysed two ancient crystalline salt reservoirs where in both cases the local populations have proved to be highly resistant to many of the modern diseases to which of those of us on western diets succumb.

The use of these salts is an essential part of the longevity programme, particularly since they will "top up" your depleted reserves of trace elements, improve electron transport along the metabolic pathways of your body, improve kidney and liver function and help alleviate any joint pains that you may have accumulated and which accelerate ageing.

Multiple interactions.

Only recently has medical science accepted how tightly the human body and nature are interlocked   The surge of 20th century technology deluded us into thinking we could capture nature in a test tube. Now we know we can't.

Now we know there is never a deficiency of just one vitamin or mineral. There is never any vitamin or mineral activity by itself!

The multiple interactions of these essential subjects is the basis of their biological function and the adequacy of that function depends on the substances being supplied to the body in the same mixtures and concentrations that occur in raw, unprocessed foods. It is by the use of these foods that genesis over millions of years of evolution, developed the precise mechanism to deal with them.

In other words, every nutrient and essential trace element operates by multiple interactions.

The 85 plus trace elements available in these ancient sea salts are vital to the operation of the equivalent hormones in our bodies. Therefore, there is a direct correlation and since our hormones dictate our moods, we are unbalanced emotionally and mentally by the lack of some, if not most, of these elements in our diet in the proportions with which we evolved with them.

VITAMIN C.

Vitamin C is essential to life and as we saw in the talk on iodine/cyanobacteria/oxygen, Vitamin C is the mechanism by which life was able to use oxygen and thereby to vigorously proliferate.

Vitamin C or L-ascorbic acid, is a rather simple substance, its chemical formula being C6H8O6. It's closely related to carbohydrates; indeed in the cells of plants and most animals (with man being one of the exceptions) it's made from the simple sugar glucose (dextrose, grape sugar, corn sugar), which has the formula C6H12O6 (not a lot of difference). Ascorbic acid is a weak acid with an acidic strength between that as citric acid (the principle acid in citrus fruits) and acetic acid, the acid of vinegar. More importantly, it's also a chemical-reducing agent capable of combining with oxygen and serving as an anti-oxidant. As an anti-oxidant it's effective, together with Vitamin E, in protecting cell membranes against damage by oxidation.

In addition to this function and its function in the synthesis of collagen, it's involved in a host of other bio-chemical processes in the human body.

Vitamin C is essential to the mechanism of life because it can easily pass one of its electrons to oxygen. When it does this, it's remaining structure becomes destabilised and is known as a very reactive free radical. This is a molecule that's lost an electron and needs to absorb another as quickly as possible to get back into balance. It does this by taking an electron from the methylglyoxal attached to the protein. (You remember I mentioned methylglyoxal as a very very early mechanism of electron transport which developed shortly after life got started on this planet). By taking an electron from methylglyoxal, this enables the protein to pass more electrons down this chain to the oxygen. This gives rise to a much higher level of electronic activity than could otherwise take place.

Electron transport.

This bridge from the protein to the methylglyoxal to the Vitamin C to oxygen, is basic to most life on this planet, and acts both as a bridge and an essential buffer. The reason for this is that if oxygen could take electrons straight from protein, we'd burn up in rapid oxidation. As it is, it's a regulated process requiring lots of Vitamin C.

In this pivotal role, Vitamin C is different from all of the other vitamins and since we don't get nearly enough in our food, it's essential that you take a Vitamin C supplement. Everybody's metabolism is different to the extent that some of us appear to be almost different species from others (this is not the case) having different digestive systems and different internal layout. However, the minimum intake of Vitamin C to remain fully healthy and to have one's blood fully oxygenated is 3,000 milligram a day and for other individuals it's 10,000 milligram a day. This can only be established by trial and error (or blood tests) but is vital to both the immune system and to longevity.

Concerning the immune system, T-lymphocyte cells are our main mechanism of cellular immunity. Keeping the T-cells in top condition is critical to the prevention of ageing. They protect the body against foreign cells, bacteria, fungus, virus and allergens and they also help the body resist cancer and auto-immune diseases. Defective T-cell function accompanies most degenerative diseases including cancer, rheumatoid arthritis, multiple sclerosis, diabetes mellitus and ulcerative colitis.

A big part of the ageing process is the gradual decline in T-cells which occurs even without any apparent disease. T-cells have a very high level of Vitamin C but with age degeneration the level drops progressively and we lose our resistance to disease. The Vitamin C level of T-cells and companion white cells, is essential in fighting disease because if you do get a virus or other infection, it drops very quickly.

The more severe the infection the worse the loss, unless you take a C supplement. Dietary Vitamin C reduces the loss of Vitamin C in the T-cells and can considerably reduce symptoms.

Moreover concerning the use of oxygen, blood volume and red blood cell counts vary with exercise and with the help of Vitamin C, new capillaries grow in the heart and skeletal muscles to carry the improved blood supply. Accordingly, there's a huge improvement in performance since the Vitamin C helps balance the pH of the blood which is then made more alkaline. An alkaline bloodstream is capable of carrying considerably more oxygen than an acidic one and I'll deal with this later when I come on to alkalinity.

About Vitamin C intake.

Vitamin C cannot be stored in the body, it's got to be replenished regularly. However, the blood will only absorb so much Vitamin C regardless of how much you may take at one time. For example, I take between 5 and 8 grams a day and how much is excreted will depend on my body's specific need at that time.

When I'm under stress I need more Vitamin C and at other times perhaps less.

This intake will rapidly cause deep saturation and then will taper off gradually returning to the previous level, so that since Vitamin C is inexpensive, it's better to waste a bit than to take too little. Vitamin C has improved beyond any doubt to be totally non-toxic and since its discovery by Albert Szent-Györgyi, abundant research has proved its efficacy.

In 1970 after the publication of Linus Pauling's book on the treatment of the common cold, Vitamin C became a temporary fad, but when Linus Pauling (two-time Nobel prize winner) and doctor Ewen Cameron published their three studies on the importance of Vitamin C in cancer treatment, it has been roundly attacked and many attempts have been made to discredit its usefulness by a pharmaceutical industry which cannot patent it and therefore cannot profit from it.

<u>The animal kingdom</u>.

Because of a 60 million year old genetic defect, humans have been deprived of the ability to make their own ascorbate in their livers. Plants manufacture their own Vitamin C with great efficiency. Animals are also able to make their own Vitamin C, with three great exceptions:-

The fruit bat, the guinea pig, and the primates; monkeys, apes and you and I!

It seems ironic that a goat, which is similar in weight to a man can manufacture 13 grams of Vitamin C daily (and double, even quadruple that amount under stress) and yet you and I are left dependent upon food for our Vitamin C supply. Unwittingly nature dealt us a grievous blow.

How did this happen?

I believe that our distant ancestors were living in areas with a plentiful supply of fruit. They could eat so much fruit at that time that nature decided they got all the Vitamin C they needed in their diets. Because there seemed to be no point in the body's manufacturing Vitamin C, that ability was lost since it makes no sense to nature to carry around the hardware for providing the enzyme L-gulonolactone oxidase if it's not needed.

Unfortunately, from a biological standpoint, we no longer live in a jungle where we can walk up and pick a piece of Vitamin C rich fruit whenever we feel hungry. This is a tragic turning point in our development, made worse by the fact that it's left us with an inborn desire for sweets, which was put there by nature to make sure we ate fruit that was ripe (and took in a good supply of Vitamin C).

Our bio-chemistry is the loser. We fail to get the massive amounts of Vitamin C nature intended us to have and we get fat through eating too many sweet things.

Vitamin C - an essential food.

Mankind can't get enough Vitamin C from his ordinary diet and not even from a very fruit-rich diet. The reason for this lies in the physiological difference between animals and plants. There is a difference here between animals and humans, insofar as animals manufacture large amounts of collagen which is their principle micro-molecule (in place of the cellulose manufactured by plants), and ascorbic acid is required for the synthesis of collagen.

Therefore animals need ascorbic acid in greater supply than plants do as one of the basic building blocks of their bodies. Accordingly, any animal strain which lacks the ability to synthesise ascorbic acid would probably die out very rapidly as the supply of the plant-food diet would not fulfil its needs. Since animals can manufacture Vitamin C in their bodies, they are able to apply this to the manufacture of collagen, whereas we humans cannot. Accordingly, we have to get it from our diet and by checking the amounts of several Vitamins present in 110 raw, natural plant foods, the amounts of vitamins corresponding to one day's food for an adult turn out to be (for several vitamins) about three times the usual dietary intake!

But for Vitamin C the amount in plant foods is 2,300 milligram, which is 51 times the average intake in an ordinary diet. This indicates very strongly that we all ought to be vegetarians but also there's something very special about Vitamin C.

The average amount of Vitamin C in a day's ration of 8 foods with the highest content is 12,000 milligram and our early ancestor who lost the ability to synthesise ascorbic acid was probably living in a tropical valley where these and similar high C foods provided this large amount of the vitamin.

The other primates have, for the most part, continued to live in tropical areas where the food has a high concentration of Vitamin C, but human beings have spread into other areas and their intake of Vitamin C has decreased to such an extent as to cause the health of nearly every person to suffer.

We also suffer from hypoascorbemia, a deficiency of ascorbate in the blood, or in other words the lack of Vitamin C. Accordingly, when we spread out from the jungles of Africa a couple of hundred thousand years ago, we passed the pivot point or turning point where we became shorter-lived and congenitally less healthy because our external supply of Vitamin C was dramatically reduced. Human beings with a high intake of Vitamin C manufacture more antibody molecules than those with a lower intake and antibodies or anti-toxins are protein molecules that have the power of recognising "not self" cells and combining with them, thus helping to mark them for destruction by the body's normal processes.

Self and not self.

There is another complex of protein molecules called complement that is involved in an essential way in the process of destruction of foreign cells and malignant cells. It's been shown that an increased intake of Vitamin C significantly increases the amount of the first component of complement C1 esterase, without which the whole complement cascade is inoperable and the "not self" cells could not be destroyed. That Vitamin C is required in man for the synthesis of C1 esterase is proved by the fact that the component of complement contains protein molecules that are similar to the molecules of collagen which are known to require Vitamin C for their synthesis.

Albeit on leaving the jungles our diet dramatically reduced in Vitamin C, yet the diet of paleolithic man was known by research to have contained 83% of green stuff, i.e. enzyme and Vitamin C rich fresh food (whereas modern diets are enzyme poor because of cooking and preservatives, are certainly not fresh and have very little Vitamin C in them.

Later in this series I will deal with the way that Vitamin C improves reception and function of the human antenna, but for the moment I want to turn now to the effect of Vitamin on cardiovascular disease, eye sight, atherosclerosis, chronic scurvy and cancer.

Scurvy.

Pioneering research into the relationship between Vitamin C deficiency and heart disease began in the late 1940s not long after the structure of Vitamin C was determined. Canadian doctors proved that a Vitamin C deficiency causes the condition, commonly called atherosclerosis. These doctors found that the condition will arise in 100% of Vitamin C deprived animal test subjects that don't make their own Vitamin C.

Furthermore, these Canadian pioneers demonstrated that Vitamin C alone reverses atherosclerosis in laboratory animals. (G.C. Willis, *"The Reversibility of Atherosclerosis"* Canadian Medical Association Journal Volume 77 July 15th 1957, pages 106 – 109).

SCURVY.

Heart disease is a misnomer. The disease is characterised by scab-like build ups that slowly grow on the walls of blood vessels. The underlying disease process reduces the supply of blood to the heart and other organs, resulting in angina, "heart cramp", heart attack and stroke. The correct terminology for this disease process is "chronic scurvy" a subclinical form of the classic Vitamin C deficiency disease. The findings of the Canadian team led by G.C. Willis MD were confirmed in the late 1980s by the world's then leading scientist, Linus Pauling PhD (1901 – 1994). Pauling alerted the word in lectures, in writings and on video after he and his associates conducted experiments that confirmed the Willis findings. To date this alert has never made its way into a mainstream media outlet and cardiologists are taught routinely to tell their patients that there is no connection between Vitamin C and heart disease.

From a scientific standpoint if a medical doctor or anyone tries to challenge the true nature of cardiovascular disease, they must be able to cite experiments that refute the Pauling/Willis chronic survey hypothesis. Such experiments have never been published!

The knowledge that heart disease is a form of scurvy has been suppressed from the time that the first series of Willis articles are published in the Canadian Medical Association Journal in the early 1950s. Inexplicably since the 1950s, no article favourable to Vitamin C and its connection with atherosclerosis have appeared in reputable medical journals that's widely read by medical doctors.

The Linus Pauling video.

In a 1992 lecture recorded on video, Dr. Linus Pauling explained the reason atherosclerosis forms on the walls of arteries when Vitamin C is deficient. He explained how a specific form of cholesterol causes plaques, compensating for low levels of Vitamin C, and why this discovery of a rapid cure for chronic scurvy includes the amino acid lysine. There's no doubt that the news of this cure has been suppressed, otherwise most of the public would have learned that twice Nobel prize winner Linus Pauling has suggested it. In fact Linus Pauling made the claim of an outright cure for heart disease using Vitamin C at that time.

Débâcle over cholesterol-lowering statin drugs.

Cholesterol-lowering statin drugs have become the top selling class of prescription drugs with most people reaching middle age now being routinely put on these drugs as a preventive measure.

Vitamin C, which is a fraction of the price of statin, has the very same cholesterol-lowering property as the statin drugs and Vitamin C is a powerful anti-cholesterol agent. The Vitamin C molecule inhibits the same enzyme (HMG CoA reductase) that the cholesterol-lowering statin drugs inhibit and the big advantage is that it does so without depleting the body's supply of coenzyme Q_{10}. This blockage of coenzyme Q_{10} synthesis is a serious action for statins that cause fatigue, muscle pain and skeletal myopathy (a grave deterioration of muscle). All advertisements in Canada must carry the code Q_{10} statin depletion warning, but this fact is not widely publicised elsewhere.

Transient global amnesia.

Former NASA astronaut and USAF flight surgeon Duane Graveline MD believes that the statin drug lipitor caused his own case of transient global amnesia, a statin drug associated memory dysfunction (and this happened whilst flying!). He has written a book, Statin Drugs; Side-Effects and the Misguided War on Cholesterol.

Chronic scurvy verified by cardioretinometry and reversed with Vitamin C.

It's long been known that human arteries weaken without Vitamin C and other necessary nutritional support. Dr. Pauling and associates theorised with Willis that such plaque formation will serve to strengthen arteries because they appear most often where the blood pressure is highest. This condition is most properly characterised as chronic scurvy.

Dr. Sydney Bush DOpt of the United Kingdom discovered that atheromas can be reversed in those patients instructed to take from 3,000 milligram to 10,000 milligram Vitamin C daily (the amount depending on the effect on the retinal arteries). Dr. Bush made his discovery while studying eye infections in contact lens wearers. Vitamin C was being tested as a preventive measure for these infections and serendipitously Dr. Bush noted that atheromas disappeared in the patients taking Vitamin C. He reported that some patients required as much as 10,000 milligram daily to reverse soft atheromas.

Dr. Bush has invented a new diagnostic technique which he calls cardioretinometry and be believes that this method of diagnosis will revolutionise cardiology.

Dr. Bush has also promoted the idea that chronic scurvy not only exists but can be accurately measured. Eye doctors can now easily diagnose this condition by examining the microscopic arteries behind the eye before any symptoms of heart disease appear. Thanks to Dr. Bush, we now know that Vitamin C will reverse this condition in short order at the optimum dosage determined by cardioretinometry.

The atheroma of the retinal arteries is a virtually perfect surrogate outcome predictor of coronary heart disease and will continue to be so as long as the eyes are connected to the rest of the system. The modern electronic eye camera/microscopes with high definition magnification facility show the impacting of the cholesterol beautifully and also its redissolving into the bloodstream when the system is restored to balance. This is seen in arterioles, too small to be seen with the naked eye.

Dr. Bush now has evidence that even calcified "hard" plaques can be reversed over the course of two years on a high Vitamin C intake. This development throws a hammer into the government's recommended daily allowance of 60 milligram and the 2,000 milligram maximum tolerable allowance. These are nonsense.

A safe and effective answer to the most common form of heart disease – plaques forming over weak arteries – is 6,000 milligram to 18,000 milligram Vitamin C daily to strengthen the arteries. Dr. Pauling's invention of administering high dosed lysine 2,000 milligram to 6,000 milligram resolves existing plaques. This combination appears to work in most individuals within ten days with the correct dosage.

Heart Failure.

Many people experience a remission of heart failure after they adopt Pauling's Vitamin C and lysine therapy. However, there is much evidence that the cause of heart failure in most people is the coenzyme Q_{10} deficiency. This vitamin like coenzyme is required in our fuel cells, the mitochondria, in order to manufacture the body's fuel, adenosine triphosphate (ATP).

Several other vitamins are required for the human body to produce its own co.Q_{10} and humans are known to synthesize less co.Q_{10} as we age. Pharmaceutical drugs and all the cholesterol lowering statin drugs block the body's production of co.Q_{10}. Therefore it can be accurately stated that these drugs cause a form of heart disease; heart failure.

High blood pressure/hypertension.

Blood pressure normally elevates during times of stress for short periods. The higher blood pressure ensures that glucose and other nutrients enter the cells in order to aid response to the stress. It's also normal for high blood pressure to normalise after the stressful event passes.

According to discussions in the British Medical Journal, ophthalmologists have noticed that the plaques form in microscopic retinal arteries before the onset of elevated blood pressure. Pauling's therapy is an effective treatment for hypertension, as are other nutrients such as magnesium, Vitamin B6 and the amino acid arginine. Health journalist Bill Sardi believes that 200 milligram of Vitamin B6 is more effective than many prescription drugs for hypertension.

Calcified arteries.

Many heart patients have hard or calcified arteries. This makes heart attack more likely because blood vessels are unable to dilate properly in the event of a clot or blockage. The most probable cause of excess calcium building up in the arteries of the heart patients is the use of blood thinners. These prescription medications either simulate or block Vitamin K and they're routinely prescribed.

High dose Vitamin K reduces calcium in soft tissues and is considered a standard treatment for osteoporosis in Japan. The vitamin acts as a hormone and helps remove calcium from soft tissues into bone.

Heart Attack.

Strong Vitamin C/lysine fortified arteries are less likely to rupture. If there is no rupture, there will be no clot. If there is no clot, there will be no heart attack caused by a blockage of blood to the heart. World Health Organisation researchers have discovered that low serum Vitamin E is a 70% better predictor of heart attack than either hypertension (high blood pressure) or high cholesterol.

Also, KK Teo and others have discovered that a magnesium injection immediately after a heart attack saved 55% of those who would have died (British Medical Journal 303;1499-1503, 1991).

Congenital heart defects and heart damage.

Harvard medical researchers found that Vitamin C was the only one of 880 substances tested that caused heart and muscles to regenerate from stem cells.

In 1747 when naval physician Dr. James Lind first proposed that scurvy could be cured with oranges, limes and green vegetables, he was ostracized by his colleagues for tainting the noble profession of medicine with worthless folk lore.

It took another 48 years of evidence before the Navy made limes a daily ration for British sailors. The essential ingredient in limes, Vitamin C, was not isolated for another 133 years, in 1928 by Albert Szent-Gyorgyi.

At one time beri-beri was also thought to be an infectious disease. When Japanese researcher Kanehiro Takaki published evidence in the British Medical Journal Lancet in 1877 that diet could prevent beri-beri he was ridiculed. 35 years later bio chemist Casimir Funk isolated the substance in rice husk that stops beri-beri, the vitamin we now call thiamine.

This sad history continues today with pompous ridicule and an enormous lack of understanding before the acceptance of nutritional discoveries comes about.

Cancer.

Vitamin C has many actions in the body and an important one being its antioxidant activity. Whatever the mechanism, it inhibits cancer reliably with experimental animals. It also confers resistance to the progress of cancer, even after it's established in the body. Patients supplemented with Vitamin C have a death rate from cancer between 40% and 60% less than those on normal diets. This decrease in death rate gives an increased life span of 8 to 11 years.

It's a happy outcome of the Vitamin C controversy, that Dr. Pauling has, at last, convinced the National Cancer Institute of the vitamins benefits.

Vitamin E and Selenium

One other vitamin has known effects on cancer. Vitamin E is important because of its anti-oxidant activity, especially in the protection of cell membranes. Along with Vitamin C and selenium, it is also important in protecting the intestines and colon, as some of it fails to be digested and passes through the body with food wastes. As Vitamin E is fat soluble it retards putrification of faecal fat. The colon walls are therefore subjected to less potential injury.

The fact that the human organism evolved to eat large quantities of Vitamin C and E daily is indicated because part of the natural function of these nutrients from the human body is to pass through it along with food residues to directly protect the bowels and bladder from injurious effects of the body's own waste during the process of their elimination.

Vitamins excreted in your urine and faeces are not an indication of unwise over supplementation but an essential component of the body's own protective wisdom.

Selenium too has a variety of inhibiting effects on cancer and Dr. Gerhard Schrauzer has shown that selenium in drinking water of animals reduces the risk of breast cancers substantially.

In 1977 eminent British Cancer specialist Sir Richard Doll echoed the feelings of many nutritionists when he said, "I've laid particular stress on diet because I suspect that in the next few years the main advance in our knowledge of how to control cancer will come from studying this aspect in our environment".

Conclusion.

It seems to me that over the billions of years of the evolution of life on this planet and particularly over the millions of years of the evolution of human life, cancer was never very much of a problem being a disease of extreme old age. When we lived on a normal healthy diet, we simply didn't get cancer because the diet prevented it, ergo the cause of cancer is modern lifestyle and its cure is only to be achieved through nutrition.

OXYGEN.

Billions of years ago the Cambrian era was host to the most incredible burst of plant life that has ever been recorded. Such was the vigour of this growth that the oxygen content of the air reached 50% and is against the background of this highly oxygenated atmosphere that we evolved.

It's worth the mention at this juncture, that oxygen is basically a waste product of the respiratory process of plant cells and with the vast increase of plants during the carboniferous, plants were the dominant life form as they are now.

Of all the chemical elements, oxygen is the most vital to the human body. We would only survive for a few minutes without it and it is the life giving, life sustaining element. Approximately 90% of the body's energy is created by oxygen and nearly all of the body's activities from brain function to elimination are regulated by oxygen. Oxygen starvation (hypoxia) at a cellular level is the underlying cause of most serious illness today.

Falling levels.

It's recently been estimated that the air breathed by our ancestors during our long history contained approximately 50% oxygen. We can arrive at this conclusion by analysing the decay rate in buried artefacts and the oxygen content in ice core samples thousands of years old.

Two hundred years ago, just as the industrial revolution was getting into full swing, the air was composed of 38% oxygen and 1% carbon dioxide.

Oxygen levels, measured by Swiss scientists Combi Bulletin Board - the importance of oxygen www.tbims.org, in 1945 to 46 was 22% and they've been carefully monitoring it ever since. The most recent measure shows 19% oxygen with more than 25% carbon dioxide. In our major cities the oxygen level can be lower than 10% and it's small wonder then that most of us suffer from varying levels of toxaemia and low oxygen levels. Common causes for this condition include the intake of devitalised food lacking in oxygen, lack of exercise, breathing polluted air, chronic stress and shallow breathing. These result in insufficient metabolisation causing the body to accumulate waste products faster than it can eliminate them.

Metabolism.

Basically, metabolism means the rate at which an organism processes oxygen in food (based on relative body weight, respiration rate, food consumption and age). Youth is characterised by a faster metabolic rate which consumes more oxygen, and advancing years by a slower metabolic rate. Experiments in biological time assessment pioneered by Pierre Lecomte Du Nouy during the First War World demonstrates the essential relationship between oxygen and healing. Du Nouy analysed the rate at which wounds heal according to the age of the wounded and he discovered that metabolic processes reflected in the rate at which the body consumes oxygen and processes oxygen in healing, slow down with age. We subsequently discovered that this process is reversible to a degree when higher levels of pure oxygen are made available to ageing systems.

Frankenstein food

Over 70% of the food we eat nowadays contains very little oxygen and in some cases actually leaches oxygen out of our bodies. All processed food is treated to give it a longer shelf life. These industrial processes are designed by and large to prevent oxidation (to stop things taking in oxygen and going rancid). So a high proportion of the food that we eat has no oxygen in it and has been treated to prevent oxygen getting into it (for example hydrogenated fats). Add to that the fact that processed food is cooked at high temperatures and then stored, means that there is no enzymic activity in it because high temperatures and preservatives kill off all the useful digestive enzymes and drive off all the oxygen. So, starved of oxygen and the enzymes we need, our bodies are under what is called "food stress" all the time. A lack of oxygen in our blood and a sag in our enzyme energy every time we eat, coupled with a high sugar intake, means that our blood is too "sweet" (the pH is way off scale - too much hydrogen and not enough oxygen).

You may surmise that by breathing fresh air and having lots of exercise would soon raise your oxygen levels and to a certain extent it will, but because much of the air we breathe is depleted of active oxygen and because the body uses a three step process to get oxygen into the cells, then exercise and fresh air are only part of the answer.

If our cells could use oxygen directly, we would oxidise! That is to say we would burn up. So the body uses various intermediary steps, as I've described in the first lecture, in the process of supplying oxygen to ourselves.

Dr. Otto Warburg MD, who was the greatest biochemist of the 20th century, did all the ground-breaking research into respiratory enzymes, vitamins and minerals that the body requires for utilisation of oxygen in the cells. This earned him the Nobel Prize in 1931 and he also discovered how to measure the pressure of oxygen in a living cell, a very important development that led to his discovery that low oxygen concentration and pressure always presages the development of cancer. He described the actual conditions in the cells that set up and cause cancer and clearly stated the prime, most basic, cause of cancer is too little oxygen getting into the cell.

In 1966 at a conference of Nobel Laureates in Lindau, Germany, he stated that, "we find by experimentation about 35% inhibition of oxygen respiration already suffices to bring about such transformation during cell growth".

That's it! Just one third less oxygen than normal and you contract cancer!

American physicians, Goldblatt and Cameron (noted on page 535 in the Journal of Experimental Medicine 1953, 97, 535 - 552) confirm that once a cell becomes cancerous, then no amount of oxygen will return the cells respiration back to normal. However, they confirmed that it's possible to prevent a respiration "impacted" precancerous cell from becoming permanently cancerous if oxygen deficiency is stopped early enough.

pH.

pH, as we shall see later, is the balance between acid and alkaline in any substance and herein lies the true cause of hypoxia.

Human blood has a pH value ranging from 7.3 to 7.45. Blood with a pH value of 7.45 contains 64.9% more excess oxygen than blood with a pH value of 7.3.

The pH values of 7.3 and 7.45 seem almost the same but there's a big difference in the amount of excess oxygen between the two examples of blood. The pH number is an exponent number of 10, therefore a small difference in pH can mean a big difference in the number of oxygen or OH negative ions. The difference of one in pH value means 10 times the difference in the number of OH negative ions and blood with a pH value of 7.45 contains 64.9% more excess oxygen than blood with a pH value of 7.30.

According to Keiichi Morishita in his "Hidden Truth of Cancer" if the blood develops a more acidic condition, then our body inevitably deposits these excess acidic substances in some area of the body, such so that the blood will be able to maintain an alkaline condition.

As this tendency continues, such areas increase in acidity and some cells die; then these dead cells themselves turn into acids. However some of the cells may adapt in that environment. In other words instead of dying, as normal cells do in an acid environment – some cells survive by becoming abnormal cells. These are malignant cells and can grow indefinitely and without order. This is cancer.

Accordingly, the acidity of the blood and consequently its oxygen carrying ability is at the base of and is the true cause of cancer since it gives rise to the lack of oxygen which acts as a trigger.

However, to understand a further and most important aspect of oxygenation, we must move on now to ionisation.

Electric ions in the air.

Cumulative work of research scientists all over the world has shown that air electricity comes from charged molecules of gas called ions.

All matter, whether solid, liquid or gaseous is made up of molecules. Each molecule consists of a dense core comprising subatomic particles including positively charged protons. The core is surrounded by rapidly orbiting negatively charged electrons. A normal, passive, molecule of air has the same number of protons and electrons, making it electrically neutral. This normal electrically neutral molecule, is said to be "stable" or "in equilibrium". However, because an electron is 1,800 times lighter than a proton, the electron is easily displaced. An ion is a molecule that is gained or lost an electron. A negative ion is an air molecule that has gained an electron. A positive ion is one that has lost an electron.

Ions form only a small part of the air we breathe, but they are the most important part.

There are 27,000 trillion stable molecules in every cubic centimetre of air, but the number of ions varies depending on the condition of the environment. In a clean, open, country air we can expect about 1,000 to 2,000 ions per cubic centimetre. This is reduced to only a few hundred in a polluted environment or in an enclosed ill-ventilated, air-conditioned room.

Negative ions in the air give us the feel good factor, they stimulate and energise us, they also destroy air borne bacteria and mould spores. But most important of all, they supply a large component of the energy in our blood supply.

Fresh unpolluted air is alive with negative ions, which are inhaled to enter the bloodstream via the lungs, lifting flagging spirits and restoring nature's balance within us.

Every healthy cell carries a negative charge and brain function, in particular, relies as much on correct electrical signals as it does on chemical transfers. Negative ions help to conduct this vital electric current through the body to ensure optimal cellular functioning, so the power system in your body works as follows:-

<u>The mechanism.</u>

The normally functioning immune system is an effective defence against foreign infectious agents and against body cells that have become cancerous. The immune regulatory mechanisms are genetically controlled. In humans these genes are located on the short arm of chromosome 6. They regulate the different cellular components of the immune system, whose job it is to recognise and deal with foreign or damaged materials in the body. The main components of the immune system are different forms of blood cells and a complex of chemicals known as the complement cascade. Some blood cells originate in the bone marrow as what are called stem cells and become different types of blood cells as they pass into the bloodstream.

White blood cells form the most active component of the immune system and represent only 1% of the total blood volume. Red cells also play a role in the body's defence, although not as actively as the white cells. All blood cells are manufactured in the bone marrow at the rate of 200 million a day.

Red blood cells.

Red blood cells go straight into the circulatory system. They live there for about 4 months and travel round the body about 500,000 times a month. As they pass through the lungs, they absorb the negatively charged oxygen transporting this through the body and delivering it to the cells. They then absorb the positively charged carbon dioxide released from the cells and let this out through the lungs again. Red blood cells are attracted to carbon dioxide about 200 times more than they are attracted to oxygen. Because of this they are very effective cleaning up agents in the bloodstream and an important part of the immune system.

Low frequency current.

The blood circulation system basically provides a low frequency current carrying both positively and negatively charged particles to and from all the cells in the body. The cells use this power supply to perform their work.

White blood cells.

There are four main types of white blood cells produced by the bone marrow as stem cells. Two of these, are called the macrophage and the granulocyte, circulate all the time in the bloodstream. These are the prowling predators of the immune system which can recognise and attack foreign or damaged cells. The mechanism they use to do this is electromagnetic!

The regulator.

The other two types of white blood cells are called T-lymphocytes and B-lymphocytes. The B-lymphocyte cells distribute themselves around the body with the other two types and are effective in a complex reaction of all four types of white blood cells, which is controlled and mediated by the activity of the T-lymphocytes. Once T-lymphocytes become mature, they migrate to the thymus gland. The thymus gland is part of the regulatory system of the body which is controlled by the mind, by mental states. It is the thymus acting in concert with the rest of the glandular system which regulates the immune system response.

The recharge system.

As we've seen, it's the job of the red cells to carry oxygen and nutrients around the cells and to clean up the system by carrying waste products and carbon dioxide through the cleansing organs and lungs. During each cycle they pass electrons (particles having a negative charge) to the cells which use them and pass back positive charges to be disposed of in the carbon dioxide.

White cells circulating in the blood pass through the lungs in the same way as the red cells but the white cells pick up a very strong negative charge. The white blood cells absorb negative ions from the air. Negative ions are at the core of the immune response since they "charge up" the T-lymphocyte cells which use them in an oxidative burst to kill or counter bacteria, virus or all the array of cellular malfunctions which have a positive charge.

Over kill.

In some cases the T-lymphocyte oxidative burst is over the top and fails to distinguish between the cells it is intending to attack and the surrounding normal tissue. When this arises and the immune system is then basically attacking the body, then such degenerative illnesses as multiple sclerosis and etc. can set in. This is reversible.

To summarise then, over-acidity in the body caused by poor diet is the basal cause of cancer. This over-acidity is exacerbated by the daily air we breathe which, apart from being very low in oxygen, is even lower in charged oxygen particles from which our body draws much of its power supply.

Vital life.

It is vital therefore at this stage in the course that you understand the need for a good ioniser in your bed chamber, your office, your living room, your meeting rooms and anywhere else where you live for long periods. Without the input of this ioniser, you will be breathing substandard air, that is to say polluted air which your body struggles to use fully.

As you age and eat food which is low in oxygen or has no oxygen, you will begin to accumulate acidic wastes in your cells.

Since your blood supply is under-supplied with vital electrons, it will be unable to process this acidic waste. This acidic waste builds up to the point where cells begin to collapse under acidic stress and turn into potentially cancerous cells.

Cancer is fundamentally a disease of over-acidification and, in fact, most illness from which we suffer these days are the result of over-acidification of the blood.

Apart from an ioniser, in order to stay healthy and youthful, it is vital that you ingest large quantities of Vitamin C.

Blood supply.

It's useful to think of the blood supply as two flows of electricity!

Arteries carry the negative charges picked up from the oxygen into the body and the veins carry the positive charges in the form of carbon dioxide, absorbed from cells as a product of combustion/cellular energy production, back out of the body.

This process follows a three-stage route – air enters the lungs when you breathe in and the oxygen, which has a negative charge, passes this negative charge on to the blood cells in a complex process which involves Vitamin C.

Vitamin C acts as the bridge allowing oxygen to transfer its negative charge to the blood cells. Vitamin C is the best known and most efficient electron acceptor in nature and acts as a bridge between air and protein (via methylglyoxal) as we saw earlier, to transfer a charge from oxygen to blood cells. Once the blood cells have absorbed the oxygen across the Vitamin C bridge, they distribute this charge throughout the body passing through the walls of the arteries in the form of lymph (which is composed of serum) which bathes every cell of the body with oxygen-rich negative charge that the cells require as a power supply to supplement and facilitate the workings of its energy-production system (Adenosine Triphosphate production).

The mechanism by which the cells absorb the negatively-charged oxygen across the cell membrane are provided by essential fatty acids.

These polyunsaturated essential fatty acids act as oxygen magnets in the cell membrane. They attract the oxygen that's in the bloodstream and transfer it into the cell to do work. So if you don't have the proper functional essential fatty acids at the cellular level, then your cells will not absorb enough oxygen from your bloodstream and you will be that much more susceptible to cancer.

<u>ESSENTIAL FATTY ACIDS</u>.

Analysis of the western diet shows a significant preponderance of Omega 6 compared to Omega 3. Physicians and nutritionists tell us that we are therefore overdosed on Omega 6 from our food, whilst being under-supplied with Omega 3. This is nonsense, as overdosing on Omega 3 can make you more susceptible to illness as shown in the scientific calculation of the optimum Omega 6 to 3 ratio published by Cambridge International Institute for Medical Science. This paper points out that fish oil recommendations are worthless or even hazardous to health and that excess Omega 3 in any form is hazardous.

The key ratio of Omega 6 to Omega 3 in the body tissues is four to one and that the best sources of oils in these ratios are hemp and linseed.

All tissues need EFA, essential fatty acids, which must come from the diet and for most tissues through the plasma where they are almost entirely transported by lipo-proteins, mainly in the cholesterol esters and phospholipids.

In nature, with the consumption of organic and unprocessed EFAs, rather than adulterated oils and transfats, LDL cholesterol is <u>supposed</u> to be made up of significant amounts of properly functioning parent Omega 6, linoleic acid and is not supposed to be harmful. It is the natural transporter of parent Omega 6 and parent Omega 3 into the cells. Ergo, it's not essential to lower cholesterol, but it is vital to lower the intake of transfats "processed" oils.

It's worth noting that the body has no cholesterol sensor in the bloodstream because the absolute number of cholesterol is irrelevant.

Physical chemical experiments show that linoleic acid (parent Omega 6) combine twice as much oxygen and disassociates at a much higher pressure, much closer to haemoglobin, than oleic acid does. Oxygen disassociation curves for oleic acid compared with linoleic acid, Omega 6, show a 50% reduction in oxygen transfer, given EFA deficiency. In layman's speak, this simply means that if there is insufficient Omega 6 in your diet, then the oxygen will not enter your cells, which will suffer hypoxia.

The leading authority on this, Brian Peskin, adjunct professor at Texas Southern University, has shown that huge numbers of Omega 6 based cooking oils are ruined by commercial food processing and that in the body these are incorporated into the LDL cholesterol. With the consumption and transport of defective, cancer causing processed oils, the LDL cholesterol acts like a poison delivery system. He's further shown that it's primarily the oxidised (adulterated) parent Omega 6 that clogs the arteries, not saturated fat.

Conclusion.

It is axiomatic that if insufficient fresh, oxygen-rich Omega 6 and Omega 3 essential fatty acids are transported into the body, then the body's electrically charged bloodstream will not be able to transfer its charge into the cells along with the oxygen and the result will be cellular hypoxia and rapid ageing.

CHOLESTEROL

The human body is composed of approximately 100 trillion cells, all of which need essential fatty acids for their oxygenation.

We are wrongly taught that ingesting lots of fish oil will protect us from heart disease and cancer and this is a mistake. Fish oil supplements can significantly decrease the effectiveness of your immune system and thicken your arteries. The essential fatty acid that we need most of all is parent omega-6, best found in hemp oil since parent omega-6 is a much better oxygen mop and can therefore oxidise the cells much more efficiently. The secret to good health and weight loss is the proportion of omega-6 to omega-3 in our diet and it is proven beyond doubt that whilst we get enough omega-3 from a normal diet, we don't get anything like enough omega-6.

Because omega-6 thins the blood thus increasing blood speed and viscosity, it cuts down the amount of cholesterol that builds up in the arteries allowing healthy levels to remain.

Contrary to what we are told, cholesterol which is manufactured by the body is a very useful substance since it is used to strengthen weakened arterial walls and for other functions in the body. Where medical science has, until recently, been fooled by the research, fooled into thinking that cholesterol was necessarily bad for you, it's because no real analysis of high cholesterol diets have been properly undertaken. A very good example of this are Eskimos who have a very high cholesterol diet and do not suffer from heart disease. A yet better example is the Japanese who have a very low cholesterol diet and suffer from extremely high levels of heart disease!

One of the main causes of obesity is not the amount of fat we eat but what that fat contains and what that fat can do within our cells.

Almost all fats in our diet have been denatured, contain an array of additives to "preserve" them from oxidation and/or are cooked at high temperatures, thus removing all the oxygen.

The main cause of obesity in our society is the ingestion of vast amounts (relatively speaking) of processed fats.

These fats containing no oxygen cannot be utilised by our bodies and are therefore stored in our adipose tissues. (This is one of the body's mechanisms for dealing with toxins).

Fundamentally, we are being poisoned by our high processed fat diet and will continue to be so as long as food processing denatures all of the fats involved.

To revert to the omega balance, the proper parent omega-6 to omega-3 ratio in the human diet is critical. Overdosing too much parent omega-3 (fish oils, flax oil and so forth) will force an excess into the tissue. Ingestion of more unprocessed parent omega-6 (unprocessed hemp oil) likewise alters, although for the better, the cells membrane composition, allowing more oxygen to pass into the cell helping it to function correctly. To "switch off" the obesity response, it is necessary to cut out processed foods from the diet, cut out all processed fats and replace these with a supplement of 3 teaspoons-full of hemp oil (one with each meal) each day.

This will have the effect of thoroughly and properly oxygenating the cells, thinning the blood, reducing inflammation and reducing the body's fat load. It will also reduce what are misnamed cholesterol levels (these being basically an excess of unprocessed fats in the body) and return you ultimately to a normal body mass index. All of the research substantiating the foregoing is available from the website of Professor Brian Scott Peskin http://www.BrianPeskin.com

RETURN TO THE SEA.

Human beings are the only true bipeds on the planet and our spine is unique amongst hominids in that it has both primary and secondary curves. The primary curve came into being when our first primitive ancestors made the transition from the deep to the shallow sea/shore line and its purpose was to lift our vital organs off the ground and assist rapid locomotion.

Between the development of the primary curve and the secondary curve millions of years passed. During this time, we developed into hairy hominids, like all the other apes, and developed thick coats of fur which is far the best dry-land insulator in hot climates. Our body hair way back then served a dual purpose, it acted as a thermal protection system. It cooled us down deflecting the heat from the sun by preventing its rays from reaching the skin. This reduction of the heat load is comparable to moving from direct sunlight into the shade and is why desert dwellers such as the Bedouin cover their heads and bodies from the heat of the sun.

Paradoxically, that same body hair also fulfils a contrary protective function when night falls on the Savannah and it gets very cold, it creates an insulating space which protects against the loss of body heat.

Our lack of hair and our upright posture indicates a major turning point in our evolution and this came about when we went back to the sea for several millennia.

Our hominid ancestors were driven to seek the shelter of the sea about the same time as the dolphins went back into the sea and this came about because of a period of excessive solar flares when radiation jumped and much of the land mass in the tropics became too hot to support life easily. Obviously, many species did survive this transition on land and these are dominantly made up of species that in those days burrowed beneath the surface or lived on the water margins in the cooler northern and southern climates.

The secondary curve.

The secondary curve in our spine came about when we lived in the shallow seas which then existed in north eastern Africa moving into the sea and out of the sea in a diurnal rhythm. The secondary curve developed when we began to lift our heads up from the surface of the sea to keep in touch with our environment. We developed our upright posture when our bodies were supported by the water. In time our pelvis rotated forward and the billions of neural connections were made which enabled the development of intrinsic equilibrium in the spine so as to enable us to walk upright on land. This proved to be a major evolutionary advantage, since walking upright on land gave us the ability to see much further and it's around this time that our binocular eyesight developed its fine degree of acuity we enjoy today.

Hairy hominids.

Despite the evolutionary advantages that living on the sea shore and in and out of the sea conferred upon us, we would never have survived unless we simultaneously acquired a mechanism to maintain our core temperature at a fairly constant 96 degrees Fahrenheit. It maintains this irrespective of the fluctuating temperatures from blazing heat to freezing cold, of the external environment.

The system that we evolved involves a vast network of blood vessels beneath the skin whose dilation or contraction directly affects the loss (or conservation) of heat within the body. This system is supplemented by the powerful heat dissipative effects of the copious secretions produced by the sweat glands and according to the biologist, William Montagna, no other species has a comparable labyrinth of blood vessels under the skin.

So basically, we transmuted or withdrew our fury coat beneath our skin where it formed a labyrinth of blood vessels in what became our subcutaneous blubber. This evolutionary step can be seen in dolphins and whales and in fact in most other sea mammals. A temperature-sensitive mat of blubber being the best way to insulate oneself in water.

What I'm not saying here is that we became fully functioning sea creatures again, but what I am saying is that we had daily recourse to the sea for protection and probably for sustenance during a time when life was extremely taxing in the interior.

The fact that we retain the hair on our heads and faces (in the case of the male of the species) is a good indication that our heads were free of the water much of the time and the fact that we retain hair on our genitals and under our arms is a good indication that these are areas where the sweat needs to be wicked away when on land.

Greater sensitivity.

Hair in all creatures acts as a very sensitive antenna, a fact which has been proved by American Indian Scouts serving in the Army.

Out on the prairie or in the forests, those scouts who had not cut their hair were able to detect the presence of somebody sneaking up on them much earlier than those scouts who had the standard American Army hair cut!

This probably accounts for much of the sensitivity of animals which retain their hair and who are clearly able to perceive a threat over considerable distances.

Stripy.

There are several sets of lines on the human body which don't follow nerves, vessels or lymphatics. They don't correspond to or conform to any known anatomical basis but they're remarkably consistent across the human race. These lines are called Blaschko's lines and were first drawn by Blaschko 75 years ago. As I've said, they've no known structure except that skin diseases frequently follow these patterns. (These lines are not to be confused with Voights lines and Langer's lines and the lines of innovation of the spinal nerves). These clearly have a purpose on the human body, whereas Blaschko lines do not appear to, on the surface of things.

Blaschko lines, however, do follow the lines of separation which water takes when impacting on or leaving the human body. It's interesting to note that on the surface of the skull the Blaschko lines follow the vortex of energy along which the hairline grows.

I offer this observation that the Blaschko lines may well be the result of our long-term regular immersions in the sea, especially since nature never does anything without a purpose.

BLASCHKO LINES

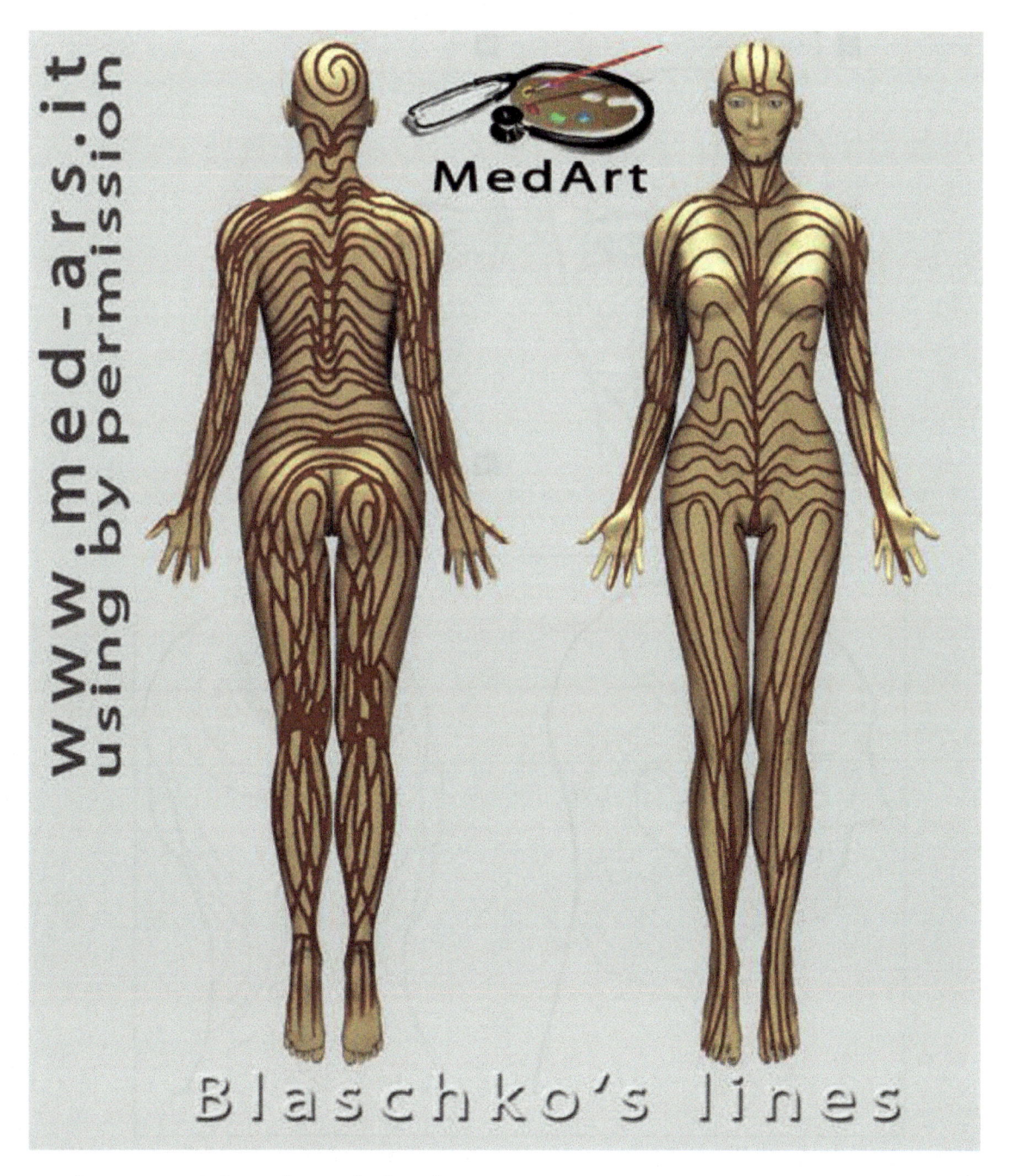

MedArt copyright acknowledged

59

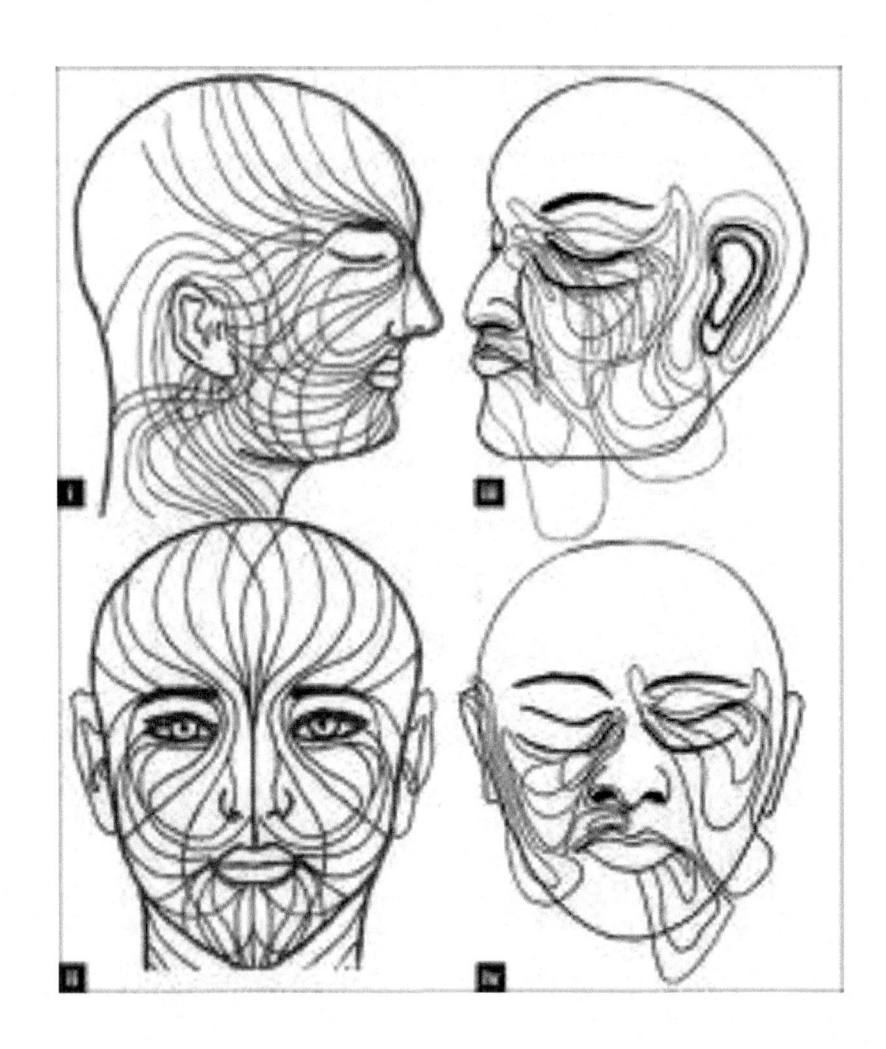

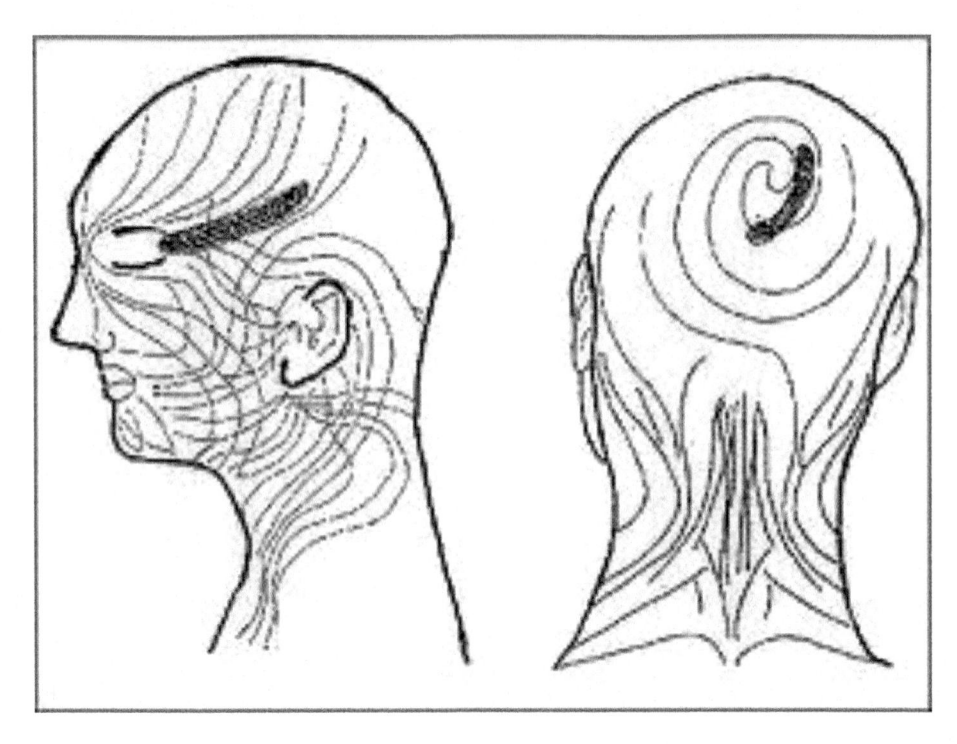

WATER.

Having come from and enjoyed a very long-term relationship with the sea, it's not surprising to learn that the human body requires three litres of clean pure water a day to function properly.

Human adults lose approximately 2.7 litres of water daily as a waste excreted through the skin, lungs, kidneys and digestive system.

Some fluid is made by the body whilst it's working on our behalf (14%), the rest must be taken in daily, mostly from drinks (52%) and the remainder (34%) from food. A little and often is better as the water is able to soak into tissues to help dissolve and excrete waste products.

Dehydration causes insomnia and tiredness, hypertension and headaches, arthritis and heart problems, high cholesterol and dementia.

The best time to drink water are one glass one half hour before taking food – breakfast, lunch, and dinner – and a similar amount 2½ hours after each meal. This is the minimum amount of water your body needs.

Water and ageing.

With increase in age, the water content of the cells of the body decreases, to the point that the ratio of the volume of the body water that is inside the cells to that which is outside changes from a figure of 1.1 to almost 0.8. As we age we tend to drink less water and become dehydrated, partly because we lose our thirst sensation progressively from the age of 40.

Besides being a solvent, water in the body is a means of transport. It has a firmly established and essential hydrolytic role in all aspects of the body metabolism – water-dependent chemical reactions. At the cell membrane, the osmotic flow of water can generate hydroelectric energy (voltage gradient), that is stored in the energy pools in the form of ATP and used for elementor (cation) exchanges, particularly in neuro-transmission. ATP is a chemical source of energy in the body which water helps manufacture.

Water also forms a particular structure pattern and shape that seems to be employed as the adhesive material in the bondage of the cell architecture. There exists small water ways or micro-streams along the length of the nerves that float the package materials along guidelines called micro-tubes. In a dehydrated state, the proteins and enzymes become less efficient and it follows that water regulates all functions of the body.

Water in a living body.

Dr. Moo-Shik Chun, Professor at Korea Science and Technology Institute in Seoul has described one protein molecule as being surrounded by 70,000 water molecules which form at least three different layers with different structures. Classified as x, y and z layers, the watermolecules closely attached to the protein molecule form what is called the z layer water and the furthest layer is the x layer which is more like the bulk water outside the body. The layer in between is called the y layer. The z layer water is ionically bonded with the protein molecule and is very much restricted. It's almost like solid water but will not freeze until the temperature is very low.

On the other hand, the bulk water, the x layer, is quite free from the influence of the protein molecule and freezes at zero degrees centigrade. The y layer water freezes at around minus 10 and the study of this layer is important to be able to understand the health and the enzyme activities in the living organism. For example, the y layer surrounding an alanine dipeptide molecule has 62% hexagonal structures, 24% pentagonal structures and 14% other structures. Therefore it can be shown that hexagonally structured water is the water that living organisms like, which may explain the fact that snow-melted water with its high content of hexagonal structures is good for the growth of plankton, green algae and etc.

Other properties of water.

Water can retain some degree of memory. Any shortage of water will result in the capillary bed of blood vessels in the surface area of our body starting to close down. This happens when the volume of the blood is decreased by dehydration and basically the water we drink ultimately has to get into the cells. Water regulates the volume of a cell from inside and salt regulates the amount of water that is held outside. This is a very delicate balancing act and the body maintains its composition of blood at the expense of fluctuating the water content in some cells of the body.

When there's a shortage of water, some cells will go without a portion of their normal needs and some will get a pre-determined rationed amount to maintain function.

When we lose the thirst sensation (or do not recognise the other signals of dehydration) and drink less water than the daily requirement, the shutting down of some vascular beds is the only natural alternative to keep blood vessels full.

Vasoconstriction and dehydration go hand-in-hand and in persons who do not drink sufficient water fail to understand that the only other way the body has to secure water is through the mechanism of keeping sodium in the body. Thus when diuretics are given to get rid of the sodium, the body becomes more dehydrated and hypertension is the result.

Water by itself is the best natural diuretic and an adequate diet of water can prevent hypertension, heart failure, bowel cancer, diabetes, and indeed a whole range of related illnesses.

We lose our thirst reaction progressively beyond the age of 40 because of the decline in our bicarbonate levels!

Drinking coffee, tea, soda is not a substitute for the purely natural water needs of the daily stressed body. Whilst it's true that these beverages contain water, they also contain caffeine, alcohol, sugar, salt, bromine and a whole range of chemicals which are dehydrating agents that get rid of the water they're dissolved in, plus some of the water from the reserves of the body.

The authority on this subject is Dr. F. Batmanghelidj, whose book, "Your Body's Many Cries for Water" can be accessed on the internet.

Magnetic Water.

When subjected to a magnetic or an electric field, the properties of water change. Surface tension increases and structural activities linger for some time. In this way water can be imprinted i.e. fixed with a memory which affects what it passes through.

Even without this activity, one in ten million parts of water molecules are ionised and these ions in turn ionise minerals in the water to create an active chemical reaction. As water causes ionisation and thereby the flow of electrons in the water, without it our body would die because its chemical reactions would come to a halt.

To conclude this paper, the cleanliness of the water content of our cells regulate their efficiency as oscillators and thus their response to the base signal. The base signal is what maintains our energy (life flow). Therefore, the cleaner the cell, the better its reception of the signal and the longer its coherent function, the longer your life.

Finally, to return to water:-

Humankind covered the globe by expanding along seashores and up rivers. We always look out to sea and are emotionally connected to its tides.

WATER 2.

Dihydrogen oxide which we know of as water is a most extraordinary substance. When cooled, it contracts by about 10% to a point at plus or minus 4 degrees C (known as the anomaly point) when it begins to expand. By the time it has formed a solid – ice, it has become almost 10% more voluminous than it was before, so it floats!

If it weren't for this property, the lakes and oceans would freeze from the bottom up and life on earth would become extinct. Ice keeps them liquid by holding the heat in.

Water's chemical formula is H_2O. One largish oxygen atom with two smaller hydrogen atoms attached to it. The hydrogen atoms being positively charged cling tightly to their negatively charged oxygen atom and also make casual bonds to other water molecules, briefly pairing and then moving on. Every water molecule changes partners billions of times a second which is why water molecules stick together to form bodies like puddles and lakes. At any given moment, only 15% of them are touching which is why they're fairly easily separated, for instance when someone dives into a swimming pool.

In one sense, the bond is very strong which is why water molecules can flow uphill when siphoned. It is also why water has surface tension – the molecules at the surface are attracted more powerfully to the molecules beneath them than they are to the air molecules above – this creates a sort of membrane that insects can float or walk on.

Water is a superb insulator against heat or cold because, amongst its many other peculiarities, its specific heat curve is not exponential. In other words, it takes a lot of energy to move the temperature of water up or down and the energy required varies depending on its current "resting" temperature.

This is why central-heating systems cost so much to run and take so much energy to heat up from cold.

You can test this anomaly yourself by filling two containers with water, one very hot and the other cold. Drop an ice cube into each and time how long each takes to melt. You'll be surprised at the result!

Heat is embodied in the activity of the electrons which orbit the nucleus. When a substance heats up, the activity of its electron becomes more marked.

Since electrons are negatively charged bodies, their heat-enhanced activity increases the electromagnetic field of the hydrogen atoms which causes an alteration in the relative position of the oxygen atoms increasing the bond angle between the two hydrogen atoms by drawing the oxygen atom closer to them.

This increases the number and frequency of the casual bonds that the hydrogen makes to other water molecules, thus increasing the water's conductivity. Conductivity is a function of electron activity and so it is that the warmer water can freeze faster than the cold water.

CHLORINATED WATER.

In the developed countries, sand filtration of water is used to filter out most cholera bacterium and chlorination to kill the typhoid causing bacterium, salmonella typhi. Chlorine has kept western societies free of most water borne infections since the 1900s but side-effects of widespread chlorination (and more recently fluoridation) suggest that we should look at other methods of protecting ourselves from both the diseases (cholera and typhus etc.) and from the solutions (chlorine and fluoride). Both chlorine and fluoride are halogens and there is a growing body of evidence, particularly from Dr. Van Kirk, Executive and Scientific Director of the Alliance of Natural Health, and Dr. Barry Durrant-Peatfield, a thyroid specialist, which indicates that halogens are linked to the rise in obesity. Fluoride and chlorine are enzyme disruptive and affect thyroid hormones. As a result of this people can develop underactive thyroids. Dr. Durrant-Peatfield points out that thyroid problems are becoming more common, particularly in Birmingham, and one of the reasons, he suggests, is because of fluoride in the water. In 2005, the west Midlands topped the UK fat list with 22.5% of its population classed as clinically obese, while the west Midlands and areas in Tyne and Wear are the main areas in the UK with fluoridated water. It is pointed out that thyroid hormones rely on iodine, an element in the same family as chlorine, which can displace iodine in the body, leading to problems with the thyroid gland.

Children can be particularly affected if their mother is short of iodine during pregnancy.

In the 1930s, German doctors used fluoride preparations to treat an overactive thyroid. This had a strongly depressing effect on thyroid function, so much so that many patients suffered total thyroid loss. The practice was soon stopped but manufacturers were quick to find a new role for their product and marketed it as a pesticide!

The consequence of this research indicates that we should be very careful about using fluoridated toothpaste and other dental products since these could have a profound effect on our weight and our entire endocrine system via the thyroid.

Chlorine at concentrations of 0.5 of a milligram per litre is relatively safe as a disinfectant for drinking water provided only that the water is pure, that is to say, free from other organic compounds. However, where there are organic compounds (for example bromates, fulvates or organic matter) such levels of chlorine can be very damaging because the effect of mixtures (the synergistic effect) can produce trihalomethanes, haloacetic acids and haloacetonitriles which have been associated with mutations, cancers and reproductive effects in both animal and human studies.

Research has also shown that exposure to trihalomethanes increases dramatically (by at least 50%) in hot, compared with cold, water, with the by-products being absorbed through the skin and by inhalation.

This means that exposure to poisonous by-products of the chlorination process from showers and baths may be at least if not more important than exposure from water consumed orally.

It is far from proven at this time that chlorine and fluoride do affect your weight but we're dealing with it here because it may be one of the triggers and it is something that can be quite easily avoided.

We are daily exposed to 20,000 chemical compounds which we did not evolve with! We have absolutely no idea what the long-term effects of these compounds are and we've even less idea of what their synergistic effect is (what effect they have when working together).

However, we must take on board the possibility that chlorinated water and fluoridated water may be significant factors in the enormous levels of weight gain across the population and act accordingly.

How to reduce your exposure to chlorine/fluoride

1. Avoid having very long hot showers and baths unless you have installed a full house-filtration system such as reverse osmosis which will eliminate the majority of disinfectant by-products.

2. Use an activated carbon filter attached to your shower head to reduce levels of chlorine when showering. (This will reduce the risk of chlorination by-products forming within your body).

3. Swim in salt water or ozone disinfected swimming pools whenever possible.

4. Filter your tap water before drinking it, using a system known to reduce concentrations of chlorination by-products, such as reverse osmosis. Jug filters (containing activated carbon filters) reduce

chlorine concentrations in water but may have little effect on some of the by-products.

5. Drink bottled water from a good natural source.

6. Use disinfectant by-product free water for all drinking and cooking purposes and, where possible, for washing and swimming as well.

7. When dishwashing in unfiltered tap water, use rubber gloves.

8. To remove the chlorine (gas) from tap water, fill up a jug with tap water and allow it to stand at room temperature for 2 hours. However, this will not remove chlorination by-products so it should not be drunk.

CHARCOAL.

The red Colobus monkeys in Madagascar steal charcoal from cooking fires of the locals and eat it. The larger monkeys steal from the smaller and the whole species seems to value charcoal very highly. This is entirely in keeping with hominid development since these monkeys live largely on lantana leaves which contain a high proportion of secondary compounds which are poisonous to these monkeys. Because the charcoal adsorbs the toxins in their guts, these monkeys are acting very intelligently insofar as they are removing the toxins from their main staple food.

Let's go back now a billion years to the evolution of mankind. Our early hominid ancestors were 99% vegetarian, eating leaves, roots, twigs, nuts, flowers and etc. in a continual stream of green stuff.

Almost all green plants protect themselves from predation by producing a range of secondary compounds (phenols and the like) which are, to a greater or lesser degree, poisonous to the animals which eat them.

Accordingly, what we're looking at with the Colobus monkeys is the sort of behaviour that we developed billions of years ago in response to our green diet.

Social functions.

Fire on the Savannah or in the forest is nature's way of renewing the plant life and regenerating the soil and a by-product of this fire is often charcoal.

In search of charcoal, our very early ancestors will have waited until the fires went out before invading the burnt areas to pick up and consume the charcoal and in doing so will have naturally medicated themselves by eradicating the poisons from their system, thus lengthening their lives.

Cooking.

They also developed cooking at this point in time and I will deal with this later.

About charcoal.

Everything alive on earth today is, as far as we know, carbon based. Until recently it was thought that there were only three basic types of carbon available on earth and none of those were capable of providing a structure on which life could evolve.

- Graphite is made up of carbon rings which lie in planes on one another and are easily shed, also it's too malleable and has edge contaminates.

- Diamond is too rigid and has a mono-layer of hydrogen on its surface which makes it far too hard.

- Soot, which is the most closely related carbon form to us, is formless and therefore cannot provide a structure using which life could develop.

So the type of carbon upon which life is based was until recently a mystery.

In 1985 H. W. Kroto and R.E. Smalley were looking into the atmosphere of giant red stars where it was known that carbon cluster molecules form. Among other carbon species they discovered the carbon molecule C_{60} for the first time.

This type of carbon, thought to be absent from earth at that time, is very stable and has some unique physio-chemical properties. To account for these properties, they propose that the C_{60} molecule has a geodesic-like structure, similar to the geodesic dome invented by Buckminster Fuller and shown for the first time in 1967 at the World's fair.

Consequently, the C_{60} was called Buckminster Fullerene and Fullerene became the name for a whole new family of closed-caged carbon. These are often called buckyballs. In 1999 Eiji Osawa and his colleagues at Toyohashi University of Technology in Japan, demonstrated that C_{60} can be extracted from hardwood charcoal thus revealing the earthly presence of the carbon form on which life is based. It's now thought that hardwood charcoal is entirely made up of pieces of C_{60} molecules in various sizes which goes some way to explaining its adsorption qualities.

C_{60} is hollow, like a ball, but it is only three ängstroms across which is just enough space to enclose one other atom in its structure. So C_{60}, which is pure carbon, has a form or structure which is strong, resilient and biologically active. It can combine with other elements.

However, there is another aspect to the physio-chemical properties of C_{60} which make life possible:-

It is responsive to electrical fields.

When an electrical field is applied to C_{60} its geodesic structure can transform into a spiral tube. These tubes are called bucky onions and they are capable of transmitting cellular signals at a faster rate than the cells own axon connections.

Science is just beginning to explore possibilities inherent in these nanotubes but it's now known that by activating the vast surface of C_{60} charcoal, its surface layer has become more susceptible to the intermolecular forces which bind other materials to it. These intermolecular forces are called van der waals forces.

This characteristic makes C_{60} the most bio-compatible adsorbent in nature.

Adsorption.

C_{60} activated charcoal has a unique ability to adsorb toxins. This adsorption process causes atoms or molecules of a substance to form on or bind to its surface. The tiny particles of charcoal are riddled with a network of crevices, cracks and tunnels such that the combined surface area of a 1cm cube unfolds to a thousand square centimetres!

This tremendous surface area is increased when activated by steam treatment and this combined with its capillary action and electromagnetic properties make it the indisputable champion of detoxification.

Powdered activate charcoal with a very small particle size (1 to 150 microns) translates into an internal surface area of anywhere from 500 up to 1,500 metre square per gram. This vast internal network of cages is accessed by way of pores that range in size from 2 nano metres to 50 nano metres.

In detoxifying over 4,000 substances, C_{60} works through several different mechanisms - adsorption, the most well known, acts by physically binding molecules to the charcoal in a process known as van der waal forces or chemisorption. Activate charcoal can also catalyse a number of chemical reactions such as when charcoal is used to remove chlorine from water.

A feed additive.

Charcoal is not classified as a drug or as a mineral. It is completely inert and indigestible and is in a group by itself.

Charcoal and magnetism.

By accepting a chlorophyll molecule into its structure, C_{60} enabled plants, and by accepting a ferrous molecule, it enabled animals. There's another aspect to the physio chemical properties of C_{60} which make life possible – it is responsive to electromagnetic forces.

All life on earth has throughout time been subjected to the magnetism of the planet – the geomagnetic field. This has fluctuated at times quite dramatically during earth's long history, sometimes dying away to almost nothing for long periods, at other times applying very strongly. Everything is responsive to magnetism to a greater or lesser degree and this completely ubiquitous force had a profound effect on life's beginnings. Carbon C_{60} is influenced by magnetism to the extent that when an electric field is applied, its geodesic structure can transform into a spiral tube and this spiral/helical screw-like nanotube always moves to stand at right angles to the electric field – it aligns with the magnetic field.

The shape and symmetry of the carbon C_{60} molecule, combined with its electromagnetic properties, are what enabled the transition from simple crystal to what Erwin Schrödinger described as an aperiodic crystal = DNA, the molecule of life.

Life, as we know it, has two basic shapes – the double helix – spiral of DNA and the geodesic dome of viruses.

Viruses have a duragesic structure and both life forms are based on C_{60} in one or other of its two known forms.

As we shall see later, this affinity for virus is of particular use to us.
<u>To conclude</u>.

Left-handed structures form the template of life. By passing C_{60} through an electric current in a coil, it is possible to transform the Fullerene molecule into a left-handed spiral nanotube, as we've seen. This is because of the fact that the magnetic field, which is the result of the electric current, has a left-handed spiral form. This process is known as isomerisation and reflects the polarity of the molecules.

Only left-handed molecules can be used by living structures. This is because the right-handed molecules are not recognised by the Krebs cycle (the energy pump of the body) and therefore cannot be used for energy or structural conversion.

Charcoal and longevity.

Having established that charcoal molecule C_{60} is the basic structure of all living systems, I shall now go on to explain how charcoal can extend your life quite dramatically.

C_{60} CHARCOAL AND LONGEVITY.

There is strong scientific evidence to support the view that taking charcoal can extend your life span! In one animal study, Dr. V.V. Frolkis, a famous Russian gerontologist, and his colleagues, demonstrated that the lifespan in laboratory rats increased up to 34% by feeding them charcoal in their diet. Toxins, including free radicals, are believed to play a significant role in ageing, but these "loose cannons" will form a stable matrix with charcoal in the gut until they are eliminated from the body.

Researchers concluded that the binding up of these toxins in the intestinal tract before they are absorbed or reabsorbed into the system may be one mechanism that allowed the animals to live longer and healthier. Both clinical observations of patients in hospitals and numerous animals studies have demonstrated that charcoal poses no threat to nutritional uptake.

Cholesterol.

Cholesterol is an essential nutrient that the body produces more than it requires and doesn't need to be supplemented with extra cholesterol from the diet. With most westerners taking in too much dietary cholesterol, charcoal has a valuable role to play:-

Charcoal lowers the concentration of total lipids, cholesterol, and tri-glycerides in the blood serum, liver, heart and brain. In one study reported in 1986 in the Lancet, 2 tablespoons of active charcoal taken three times a day for four weeks lowered total cholesterol 25%, lowered LDL cholesterol

41% and doubled their HDL/LDL (high density lipoprotein/low density lipoprotein) cholesterol ratio.

Microscopic tissue examination shows that a daily dose of active charcoal may prevent many cellular changes associated with ageing – including decreased protein synthesis, lower RNA activity, organ fibrosis, as well as sclerotic changes in the heart and coronary blood vessels.

It can be safely said that as an anti-ageing adjunct to total health, the above cumulative effects of charcoal upon one's blood chemistry may add up to a longer life and improved overall health.

Detoxifier.

Richard C. Kauflan BS, MS, PhD (Bio-Nutritional Chemistry from the University of Brussels) has written extensively in the field of anti-ageing. He writes, "detoxification is an ongoing biological process that prevents toxins (from infectious agents, food, air, water and substances that contact the skin) from destroying health. Chronic exposure to toxins produces cellular damage, diverse diseases, allergic-like reactions, compromised immunity and premature ageing."

A general detox plan.

To counteract these daily exposures to toxins, Kauflan recommends using active charcoal either on two consecutive days each week taking a total of 20 to 35 grams each day divided into two or three doses. (In the morning, at mid-day and before bed on an empty stomach). Or, take about 20 grams a day of active charcoal in divided doses for several months. Follow with a one month's break and resume the cycle.

Incidentally, charcoal should be viewed as an auxiliary to sound health practices, not as a back-up for intentional indiscretions.

Anti-bacterial and anti-fungal properties.

Whilst photo-chemical processes now represent the most promising methods to inactivate viruses, in their article Buckminster Fullerene and photo-dynamic inactivation of viruses, the chemist Käsermann at Kempf working in conjunction with the Swiss Red Cross, explore a new alternative, namely the use of C_{60} – Buckminster Fullerene. A molecule found in abundance and almost exclusively in wood charcoal.

They tested a water soluble C_{60} derivative for anti-viral activity and this compound showed a potent and selective activity against HIV-1 in acutely and chronically infected cells. In part this was attributed to inhibiting the virus's ability to replicate and no adverse effects to the cells were observed. In fact, this isn't surprising since scientists have long known that charcoal impregnated swabs should not be used in viral research, as the charcoal tends to shut down viral activity. This research looked into the action of C_{60}

in damaging the envelopes that protect a number of deadly viruses including hepatitis A, B, C, HIV-1 and 2 and human Parvovirus B19. This latest research represents the expanding field of charcoal in medical technology but is really a follow up to the long-known history to the use of charcoal as a native remedy for a wide range of problems.

It is of interest to note that the World Health Assembly has urged all member countries of the World Health Organisation to promote the use of traditional, harmless, efficient and scientifically proven remedies (resolution 44..34). Charcoal is just such a remedy – ubiquitous – unpatentable – easy to use – entirely safe (provided it's sourced from a reputable organisation) and unchallenged as an antidote for poisoning. The world's best biological clean up system.

SLOWER AGEING.

In a study reported in 1986 in The Lancet, patients with high cholesterol took quite a high dose of charcoal (i.e. 2 tablespoons full (8 grams) 3 times a day for four weeks). This lowered their total cholesterol 25%, lowered LDL cholesterol 41% and doubled their HDL/LDL (high density liver protein - low density liver protein) cholesterol ratio.

Microscopic tissue examination shows that a daily dose of charcoal may prevent many cellular changes associated with ageing, including decreased protein synthesis, lower RNA activity, organ fibrosis, as well as sclerotic changes in the heart and blood vessels.

As an anti-ageing adjunct to a total health programme, the accumulative effects of C_{60} charcoal upon blood chemistry may add up to a longer life and improved overall health.

CHARCOAL C₆₀

A non-medicinal food supplement which can help you be more healthy and live longer.

Charcoal C_{60} is a Fullerene, so called because of the geodesic form of its molecular structure. It is the most bio-compatible form of charcoal, being the basic carbon molecule on which life is based.

1. Diabetes.

   By adsorbing glucose from the lower intestine, C_{60} can help manage diabetes.

2. Anti-ageing.

   By adsorbing toxins from your system, C_{60} can help reduce the load on your immune system and help slow down the ageing process.

3. Acid reflux.

   By adsorbing excess acid from your stomach, C_{60} can help reduce acid reflux.

4. Irritable Bowel Syndrome.

   By transporting more oxygen into your system and thus helping to balance the pH, C_{60} can reduce the incidence of irritable bowel syndrome.

5. Gas discomfort.

By adsorbing methane and CO_2 in your bowels, C_{60} can help reduce wind pain and gas.

6. <u>Reduce the effects of hangovers.</u>

    By adsorbing the fractional distillates often present in alcoholic drinks, C_{60} can help reduce the effects of these toxins on your system and thereby reduce the effects of a hangover.

7. <u>Reduce Joint Pain.</u>

    By adsorbing excess lactic acid from your bloodstream and adding extra oxygen, C_{60} can help your joints and muscles ache less during and after exercise.

8. <u>Improve digestion.</u>

    By settling your stomach and reducing excess acid, C_{60} can dramatically improve your digestion.

9. <u>Improve breath.</u>

    By improving your digestion and taking excess methane etc. out of your system, C_{60} can improve your breath.

10. <u>Improve complexion.</u>

    By lightening the toxic load caused by food additives, E. Numbers, excess salt and sugar in your diet, your liver and kidneys, C_{60} can help improve your complexion.

11. <u>Overcome food poisoning.</u>

By adsorbing poisons from your digestive tract, C_{60} can help overcome food poisoning and help many food allergies.

12. <u>Reduce diarrhoea.</u>

    By transiting the digestive tract more slowly than food and by adsorbing many times its own weight in toxic compounds, C_{60} can help manage diarrhoea. (Taken in excessive quantities, i.e. more than 5 capsules in 24 hours, C_{60} can cause mild constipation. This can be avoided by drinking more water).

13. <u>Reduce gastric ulcers.</u>

    By adsorbing excess acid from your system, C_{60} can help manage gastric ulcers which are usually caused by excess acid penetrating the gut wall.

14. <u>Depression.</u>

    Where depression has a biological basis C_{60} can often help lift an attack.

15. <u>Reduce the effects of drug overdose.</u>

    In cases of accidental drug overdose, C_{60} can help remove these agents from your bloodstream quite rapidly and for up to 24 hours after the overdose.

16. <u>Poultice.</u>

    Remove from the capsule and wrapped in a damp cloth, C_{60} provides an excellent poultice for wounds, burns and infected sores.

17. <u>Draws poisons.</u>

    Placed over an affected or challenged organ or limb, a poultice of C_{60} can often draw the poisons out, helping to restore normal function.

18. <u>Purify water.</u>

    By emptying the C_{60} capsule into a jug of grey water and stirring it in, you can remove many toxins. Leave it standing for one hour before drinking.

19. <u>Teeth whitening.</u>

    Used as a tooth powder, C_{60} is probably the best whitener there is. It also makes for a very healthy mouth by adsorbing any toxins present as well as unwelcome bacteria.

20. <u>Reduces the after-effects of chemotherapy.</u>

    If you're receiving chemotherapy, C_{60} can help reduce the after-effects by helping remove these complex toxins from your system.

21. <u>Reduces cholesterol.</u>

    C_{60} reduces cholesterol thus reducing the need to take statin drugs which have been found to have dangerous side-effects (i.e. they block the body's production of vital Co-Q10s).

22. <u>Adsorbs toxins.</u>

    You cannot overdose on C_{60}. It is chemically inert and doesn't take part in any reactions in the body. It simply, and very effectively, adsorbs most toxins and anaerobic bacteria, effectively removing these from the body.

COOKING.

Our early hominid ancestors did not have very large brains and spent 80% or more of their waking hours foraging for food and eating. (The rest of the time they spent sleeping).

You can still see this behaviour in wild primates today and this takes us to a fundamental node point where humans split off from the hominid tree to form the beginnings of the new species which culminated in us today.

The simple reason for this is that in pursuit of charcoal to stabilise their stomachs and protect themselves from the poison inherent in their green diet, our only hominid ancestors would naturally come across the burned/cooked carcasses of animals and insects that had been trapped in the fire.

As with all curious creatures, our early ancestors will have tasted these half cooked animals and found them pleasant to eat. Remember, we're talking here about a species that would eat practically anything available and spend most of its time eating.

Initially, eating these baked creatures would have given them quite sore stomachs because of the high acid content of the meat and also because of its high hormonal charge (full of adrenaline, the fear hormone) but with a handy supply of charcoal they were not badly affected by this and could continue to consume cooked meat over long periods of time when they found it.

This was a species that already ate some uncooked meat and had a difficult time digesting it – thus the charcoal was very useful in this respect.

However, when they began to eat cooked meat, they found this very much easier to chew and even easier to digest.

Cooked meat then became a very desirable energy source for these early hominids since it provided them with abundant energy which they could process easily.

The turning point.

Because of the broad availability of cooked meat and also because of the fact that they very rapidly learnt to kill and cook it themselves, they were able to spend long periods of time digesting. Relieved of the need to continually forage and to continually eat their previously totally vegetarian diet, these clever apes began to develop a much higher series of tactile skills and reasoning skills which enabled quite rapid brain development.

This rapid brain development/capacity quickly gave them the edge over their surroundings and they began to develop tools and hunting techniques which, in a few thousand generations, enabled them to spread out from the north-east African environment they'd previously inhabited and to drift along the coastlines to populate much of the planet.

Cooked food led to a higher energy input which led to more spare time, which led to more inventiveness, which led to a larger brain capacity, which led to tool use, which led to more efficient hunting, which led to the demise of many of the larger species we came into contact with and hunting became a dominant way of life which enabled us to spread around the world.

This node point was pivotal to our development, but it carried with it one inherent drawback.

For millions of years we had developed as herbivores and fructivores which gave us a sacculated bowel. The rapid conversion to cooked meat meant a much higher incidence of illness simply because we're not structured to eat meat and meat, especially meat that has only been partially cooked, lingers in our bowels and is a source of poison as it decomposes. These poisons contribute to a whole range of diseases and a quite significant decrease in the life expectancy of our species.

The slow accumulation of these acidic poisons mirrors exactly the decline in health in humans when up to 70% of the cellular contents can be deteriorating acid waste by the time we are 50.

The fact that we no longer ingest amounts of charcoal on a regular basis simply exacerbates the situation and it's difficult to over-emphasise the role that charcoal should play in our lives.

This applies to meat eaters and, lamentably nowadays, to non-meat eaters who ingest substantial amounts of poison which has entered the food chain as pesticides, fungicides and a whole range of similar pollutants.

COOKING 2.

The rapid conversion to occasionally eating cooked meat led to a sharp decline in the overall health of our species with some short-term changes in organs such as the pancreas (more of which later). However, the advantages that this conferred outweighed the disadvantages.

For millions of years we lived on raw food. Raw or living food is uncooked and thus full of enzymes, vitamins and minerals. It really feeds the body and most people report that they instantly feel better following a raw food diet. There are roughly 80 million species on earth, about 700,000 of which are animals, and all of these species thrive on raw food. Only humans apply heat to what they eat and, on average as a race, die at or below half our potential lifespan. Humans die of chronic illness which is largely diet and lifestyle related and this is unnecessary and unfortunate since our average lifespan potential in robust wellness is about 120 years.

Microscopic burnt nutrients (resulting from heated food) are toxic to the body and, as decades pass by, the harmful effects of consuming these toxins accumulate. Cooking denatures protein, altering it, making it either unusable or less usable. Heated proteins are unavailable to the body and coagulated protein molecules tend to putrify as bacteria and feed on dead organic matter.

Protein consumed is not used as protein, but first broken down into its individual amino acids and then used to build the protein molecules that the body needs. So animal flesh products must be broken down, using up energy. Raw food has an abundance of readily available amino-acids, especially ripe fruit, vegetables, nuts and seeds.

The body has to work a lot less when creating protein from the assortment of individual amino-acids from greens, rather than the already combined long molecules of protein assembled from animal flesh. When we eat greens we take in new amino-acids freshly made by sunshine and chlorophyll. The body has a hard time making protein out of something else's amino-acids. It sometimes also receives a lot of unnecessary components that are hard to digest which would be floating around in the blood-like garbage, causing allergies and other health problems. Incompletely-digested protein fragments maybe absorbed into the bloodstream causing food allergies and immunological disorders. Scientific research proves raw food protects against cancer and heart disease and decreases toxic products in the colon. A raw, vegan diet causes a reduction in the bacterial enzymes and toxic products that have been implicated in colon cancer risk. The risk of breast cancer is also lowered.

Vitamins and minerals.

Up to 50% of vitamins and minerals are destroyed by heat. Vitamin C and B1 (thiamin) are the most susceptible. B6 (pyridoxine and pantothenic acid (B5) losses could as high as 91% in canned food. When food is treated with heat, 97% of water soluble vitamins (B and C) are lost and up to 40% of lipid soluble vitamins A, D, E & K). Minerals are altered and certain ones become less absorbable. 100% of enzymes are damaged which depletes the body's supply, draining the energy needed to maintain and repair tissue and organ systems. Tests have shown that eating food devoid of enzymes as a result of cooking, food irradiation and microwaving causes an enlargement of the pancreas and causes stress to associated endocrine glands, such as the adrenals, pituitary, ovaries and testes. The human pancreas is three times larger (compared to total body weight) than that of any other animal. Research on mice fed cooked foods revealed an increased pancreas size. Upon being fed raw food again, this was reversed and the pancreas decreased back to normal. The conclusion here is that the pancreas becomes enlarged because it's forced to keep up a high digestive enzyme output.

Fats heated to high temperatures are rendered carcinogenic. Typical frying temperature is about 400 degrees Fahrenheit and can reach up to 600 to 700 degrees Fahrenheit. Oil in deep-fat fryers (especially in the fast food industry) can be reheated to temperatures of 1,000 degrees which creates free radical activity (damaging and destroying cells). When fats and oils are heated to such temperatures, naturally occurring CIS fatty acids (those which are biologically active) are converted to trans fatty acids. These are toxic and begin to behave like saturated fat. Trans fats cannot be biologically processed.

When food is heated to lower temperatures it causes leukocytosis – white blood cell activity increases as the body perceives the appearance of cooked food as an invader! White cells maintain the purity of tissues, lymph and body fluids. They will tolerate nothing abnormal in the circulatory system. This phenomenon repeated each meal, each day, each week, each year for decades slowly but surely lowers resistance to disease and drains the immune defence response causing age-related illness and premature death. Raw fresh produce is nutrient dense, easily digested and strengthens the immune system.

It is no coincidence that since 1950, as consumption of processed foods has increased, so have cancer rates! Additionally, the effect of eating high amounts of fast food, which are nutritionally bankrupt, results in the body constantly searching for quality food (even though the stomach is full) the end consequence being chronic over eating and rampant obesity. As more nutrient-rich food is eaten, the body steadily becomes healthier and its metabolic efficiency increases, along with its ability to absorb and assimilate more nutrients. Only about half the amount of protein, if eaten from protein plant food, is necessary (via nuts and seeds) rather than from cooked animal protein. Raw food leaves us energised rather than typically tired after meals and provides us with clearer minds, memory and concentration. General energy also increases.

You can still enjoy cooked foods and be healthy to some degree by food combining. This allows the digestion to operate smoothly without food fermenting and putrefying in your digestive system. However, to aim for the ideal diet of our ancestors, which contain the minimum of 83% raw food of mostly fresh produce is our ideal state and you will age a lot more slowly and be a lot less inclined to obesity if you follow this advice as closely as you are able.

Bon appétit!

HARMONIC POWER

PART III

PROSPER

A WORD TO THE WISE

This book is written for informational and educational purposes only.

It is not intended to be used as medical advice.

©Keith Foster, April 2013

PROSPER

CONTENTS

Page Number

96	Introduction
97	Fasting – Restricted diet
103	Alkalinity / Acidity
108	pH Foods list
116	Cease to be Obese (or Fat)
118	Obesity
125	Soy – Health Food?
129	Non-Human Intelligence
137	Food and Folly
149	Sleep Deprivation
152	Magnetism and Earthing
166	The Human Antenna
181	Exercise for Longevity
188	Sunlight Slim & Sunlight Healthy
191	Living Resonances

INTRODUCTION

In Part II – Gain we saw how life on earth formed and looked at some of the mechanisms that shaped us.

In Part II, we bring this closer to the present and look at what you can do in the 'here and now' to help yourself fulfil your true potential.

FASTING – RESTRICTED DIET.

We are structured to be a hungry hominid. According to the structures of our palates and our gut, we have evolved to live on masses of raw fruit, shoots, nuts and vegetation with very occasional (and often dangerous) intakes of raw meat. We are designed with digestive systems capable of getting the very maximum energy and food value out of a wide range of diets and we are evolved to live well on very little food. Until about ten thousand years ago we lived as hunter-gatherers and the rhythms of such life meant enduring long and regular periods of hunger. We're actually structured to respond to wide fluctuations in food supply and to go hungry or slightly hungry for much of the time.

During the Second World War, when I was born, the population of England, as a whole, had to manage on very simple rations, with little in the way of processed foods. We were far more healthy than we are now (despite the appalling stresses and strains of total warfare) and it's clear from this that most illness is diet related.

This is also clear proof, if proof be needed, that almost any mental or physical stress can be borne almost indefinitely as long as the rule of simple and "spare" eating is observed.

This is really hard to come to terms with and at first it's going to take all your concentration and willpower to achieve. You must eat less, you should now eat about half of what you ate before.

Unless you are doing hard physical work, you do not need to take in large amounts of food each day. On the contrary you need to take in, to eat, small amounts of the right food regularly.

Repeatedly, in the last 3,000 years, outstanding individuals have tried to tell people about the relationship between food and health. Probably the best illustration of the link is supplied by the writings of an Italian nobleman, Luigi Cornaro of Padua who lived 400 years ago. His lively wit and longevity make his work just as relevant today as it was when he wrote it and a broad overview of his story is as follows:-

"It is in everyone's power to eat and drink what is wholesome and avoid over feeding. He that is wise enough to observe this will suffer little from other incapacities. The man who pursues a temperate life with all possible exactness will seldom, if ever, be seized with disease".

After a riotous youth, by 40 he was broken down and said to be dying. He dismissed his two doctors and resolved to overcome his intemperate ways. He's quoted then as saying: "Alas for my clever physicians – they're long dead, while I, aged 100 remain in excellent health". His final and most pithy observation is "he would eat much must eat little, for eating little lengthens a man's life and by living longer he may eat a great deal more". Cornaro died at 102 absolutely without pain sitting in an easy chair.

In a later generation, George Bernard Shaw, the great playwright, provides a similarly good example.

He had a poor body and suffered indifferent health but by abstemious eating he managed to maintain a virile mentality until the day of his death.

Processed food.

Processed and cooked food is denatured, containing very few or no enzymes and costs you a lot of energy to digest. That energy, drawn from throughout your body, leaves you weaker and more susceptible to illness. Also, and more to the point in this context, it leaves you less able to recover or fight back once you have an illness.

The correct healthy diet for human beings is ripe fruit, ripe nuts, ripe seeds, ripe vegetables, ripe salads, ripe vegetation and ripe water.

A sacculated bowel.

Looking for further corroboration of a vegetarian past, I found that uncivilised tribes living on largely vegetarian diets are not affected with cancer any more than are wild animals. Yet when these same tribesmen adopt civilised food, cancer develops. Much known information now corroborates this evidence but the chief fact is that flesh food often rots before elimination so that putrefying residues are absorbed into the bloodstream from the colon poisoning the whole system as a consequence.

This occurs a lot in humans because of the structure of the bowel. The small intestine is basically a long spiral tube with a series of sac-like or egg-shaped variations in its length. Stretched out this gives the appearance or shape of a long necklace of small lumps and these sacs have a specific job to perform.

Raw vegetation or fibrous matter is often quite high in cellulose which is difficult for our digestive systems to break down and use. To facilitate the use of this food, which in our recent past (up to 10,000 years ago) formed our main diet, we evolved a sacculated bowel. This structure slows down the rate at which our food is evacuated and allows the movement of the body to massage the lower abdomen so as to work or knead the partially digested food as it passes through the intestine. (This is why walking after a meal can help digestion). The sacculations in the bowel, evolve to aid in the digestion of simple vegetable and fruit material rich in its own enzymes, have just the opposite effect on meat! They slow it down dangerously.

All carnivores have smooth bowels. These enable them to eat fresh killed meat, full of the fear hormone adrenalin and very poorly supplied with natural enzymes. Their systems take what they need very quickly from this rapidly decaying toxic mass and then get rid of the residues very quickly through their smooth bowels so as to avoid the bulk of toxic absorption.

Untreated toxins derived from unnatural food in the bowel flood the body. This is the root cause of most illnesses.

In a study performed at the Harvard laboratories of physiology, it was shown that a meat diet produces an acceleration of the heart that's surprising in its magnitude and duration. After a meal of meat the increase of the heart rate regularly amounts to between 25% and 50% more than its previous level. This persists for 15 to 20 hours. This is the total of many thousands of extra heartbeats and it's known that it requires the presence of internal poisons to cause the body's functions to accelerate in this manner.

You were born with a finite fund of heartbeats and it is madness to go on accelerating these in this manner since you are then using up your reserve!

Fasting.

Throughout history religion and philosophy have laid great emphasis on regular fasting as a method of clearing the mind and purifying the body.

If we stop eating for a time, our bodies work away steadily and use up all the food matter available in our intestines. Everything is gradually broken down and used and this process continues until nothing is left. In this way all the cellulose and all of the other hard to use material which would normally be ejected, is broken down and used until the digestive system is thoroughly empty.

Then, and only then, does the body begin to use its reserves of stored fat and as these are processed into glucose, the toxins they often contain are dealt with by the immune system often being excreted through the skin as perspiration.

Finally, the bloodstream is cleaned of all toxins and foreign matter by the enzymes and white blood corpuscles and the body becomes completely healthy. At this point the bowel becomes completely sterile and the body becomes completely healthy.

With knowledge of the foregoing, its axiomatic that the human body is perfectly capable of clearing up almost any illness left to its own devices to do so and if all extraneous stresses are removed, or reduced as far as possible.

Begin to fast one day a week and you will notice a very rapid improvement in your health (and longevity). If you find this impossible to do, then simply halve the quantity of food that you take in at each meal and stop digging your grave with your knives and forks, chop sticks, fingers or by whatever other method you eat.

ALKALINITY / ACIDTY.

Electrons are negatively charged particles that revolve around the positively charged nucleus in a molecule. They form the basis of the flow of electricity passing a bucket-like charge along the row of molecules. This is called electron transport.

Electron transportation is the tidal flow of life in the body and performs a vital role in healing. What happens is this:-

When an injury or imbalance occurs in the body, that area becomes inflamed. This inflammation is the complex biological response of the body to harmful stimuli, such as pathogens, damaged cells or irritants. It's a protective attempt by the immune system to remove injurious or threatening agents, as well as start the healing process for the affected tissue. In the absence of inflammation, wounds and infections would never heal and you wouldn't survive.

White blood cells constantly circulate through the body on the lookout for infection or damage. As weapons, some of these cells release a burst of free radicals (this is called an oxidative burst). Free radicals are positive charged molecules (short of one or more electrons) that search for (negatively charged) electrons to become stable. They usually strip away electrons from pathogens and damaged tissue and this actively kills the bad bugs and breaks down the damaged cells for removal.

As the remedial work winds down, excess free radicals are neutralised by anti-oxidants or free electrons in the body.

However, if the inflammation caused by the pathogens etc. is long lasting (i.e. chronic) then the extra free radicals created by the immune system will begin to strip electrons from the healthy cells as well, and this can seriously harm you!

What happens then is that the immune system switches into overdrive sending more white blood cells to produce more free radicals which then progressively attack the healthy tissue.

Scientists unanimously agree that free radical activity is the basis of chronic disease and the ageing process, particularly accelerated ageing and limited life span.

One of the best ways to combat this damaging process is to supply the body with more oxygen. Now, the ability of the blood to absorb oxygen is governed by its pH. That is to say by its acid/alkaline balance. When blood is on the acidic side it can't absorb or transport enough oxygen. When it's more alkaline, it's ability to absorb and transport oxygen is very considerably increased. If we alkalise the blood then we are making much more oxygen available to the system. Since oxygen is the penultimate store of electrons, we are supplying the body with the means to shut down the excess immune response by providing the free radicals entrained by the oxidative burst with the means to regain their stable state again.

This does not reduce the immune system, but simply enables it to distinguish between damaged tissue and healthy tissue once more and so to do its job better.

The best way to regulate the immune system then is to supply the bloodstream with the correct balance of natural electrons.

pH.

A healthy body functions best when it's slightly alkaline. Deviations in the blood above or below a pH range of 7.30 to 7.45 can signal potentially dangerous symptoms or states of disease which warn us of a deeper-rooted disease process. When your solent tissues pH levels deviate from a healthy range (7.2 to 7.5) into an acidic state (below 7.0 pH), the acid waste normally disregarded through the body's elimination routes start to back up and clog the system.

Why we age.

The human body produces a balancing factor of high alkalinity which is bicarbonate (HCO_3). Bicarbonate keeps the blood alkaline. As I mentioned before, In 1996, Dr. Lynda Frassetto of the University of California, San Francisco, published a paper showing how bicarbonate levels in human blood vary with age.

The average bicarbonate level is constant until the age of 45, after which a noticeable decline begins. (This is the age when symptoms of diabetes, arthritis, hypertension, osteoporosis, cancer etc. start to appear).

Physical ageing occurs when bicarbonate in the blood decreases. As these levels decrease the body is less able to neutralise acid which accumulates as cholesterol, fatty acid, uric acid, kidney stones and etc.

WHY YOU SHOULD EAT AN ALKALINE DIET.

Various stomach lining glands produce mucous that has a pH of 7.7 and contains large quantities (up to 0.5 gram a day) of sodium bicarbonate. This alkaline mucous protects the stomach from its own acid. Bicarbonate production rises if pH falls and vice versa. Other stomach lining glands enable sodium and chloride ions to join with water and carbon dioxide to form hydrochloric acid (stomach acid) and sodium bicarbonate. For each molecule of acid produced, one of sodium bicarbonate is produced too.

All foods stimulate stomach acid production by distending the stomach, but protein is the main stimulus. Hydrochloric acid is released into the stomach but bicarbonate ions are absorbed from the glands into the blood.

Alkaline tide

Blood leaving the stomach is relatively alkaline as it's rich in bicarbonate and short of chloride. As this alkaline tide circulates round the body, its raised alkalinity helps to reduce any acidosis resulting from a meal.

An acid forming meal increases stomach acid production and any excess acid is absorbed into the blood which adds to its acid load. Conversely, when we have an alkaline producing meal, our stomach doesn't need to produce large amounts of sodium bicarbonate so it doesn't produce large amounts of stomach acid either.

Several hours after a meal the stomach contents enter the duodenum as acidic slurry.

The alkaline diet.

Whilst the average industrial age diet is acid producing, studies suggest that in pre-agricultural societies of over 70,000 years ago, 87% of people ate an alkali-producing diet.

Many experts today assert that alkali-producing foods should compose 80% of our diet with acid producing foods making up the rest.

It is this major swing in the acidity of our diet that has dramatically shortened life when we began to ingest large quantities of animal protein.

To redress this we need potassium which is plentiful in vegetables and fruits and produces strong alkalising ions in body fluids.

Conclusion.

We can deal with temporary acidosis from an occasional acid producing meal, but weeks or months of chronic low grade acidosis causes many symptoms of grave illness and dramatically shortens our lives. This has been one of the major pivots in our loss of longevity.

pH Foods List

The pH scale runs from pH 0 for very strong acid (e.g. battery acid) to pH 14 for very strong alkali (e.g. liquid drain cleaner) a pH of 7 being neutral (e.g. "pure" water).

For the purposes in categorizing foods a condensed scale has been used in the guide table, with Blue to indicate neutral (pH7); between acid red around (pH 2); and alkali green around (pH 10).

Food Category	Food	pH Rating <-- highly acidic -- highly alkaline -->				
		pH2			pH7	pH10
Breads	Corn Tortillas		x			
Breads	Rye bread			x		
Breads	Sourdough bread		x			
Breads	White biscuit			x		
Breads	White bread		x			
Breads	Whole-grain bread			x		
Breads	Whole-meal bread			x		
Condiments	Ketchup		x			
Condiments	Mayonnaise		x			
Condiments	Miso		x			
Condiments	Mustard		x			
Condiments	Soy sauce		x			
Dairy	Buttermilk				x	
Dairy	Cheese (all varieties, from all milks)		x			
Dairy	Cream			x		
Dairy	Egg whites		x			
Dairy	Eggs (whole)		x			
Dairy	Homogenized milk			x		
Dairy	Milk (not pasteurized)			x		
Dairy	Milk (pasteurized)		x			
Dairy	Paneer (cheese)		x			
Dairy	Quark		x			
Dairy	Yoghurt (sweetened)		x			
Dairy	Yoghurt (unsweetened)			x		
Beverages & Drinks	Beer	x				

Category	Item	1	2	3	4	5	6
Beverages & Drinks	Coffee	x					
Beverages & Drinks	Coffee substitute drinks			x			
Beverages & Drinks	Fruit juice (natural)			x			
Beverages & Drinks	Fruit juice (sweetened)	x					
Beverages & Drinks	Liquor	x					
Beverages & Drinks	Soda/Pop		x				
Beverages & Drinks	Tea (black)	x					
Beverages & Drinks	Tea (herbal, green)				x		
Beverages & Drinks	Water (Fiji, Hawaiian, Evian)				x		
Beverages & Drinks	Water (sparkling)		x				
Beverages & Drinks	Water (spring)			x			
Beverages & Drinks	Wine		x				
Fats & Oils	Borage oil				x		
Fats & Oils	Butter			x			
Fats & Oils	Coconut Oil (raw)				x		
Fats & Oils	Cod liver oil			x			
Fats & Oils	Corn oil			x			
Fats & Oils	Evening Primrose oil				x		
Fats & Oils	Flax seed oil				x		
Fats & oils	Hemp Seed oil				x		
Fats & Oils	Margarine			x			
Fats & Oils	Marine lipids				x		
Fats & Oils	Olive Oil				x		
Fats & Oils	Sesame oil				x		
Fats & Oils	Sunflower oil			x			
Fruits	Acai Berry			x			
Fruits	Apples			x			
Fruits	Apricot			x			
Fruits	Apricots			x			
Fruits	Apricots (dried)			x			
Fruits	Avocado (protein)					x	
Fruits	Banana (ripe)		x				
Fruits	Banana (unripe)				x		
Fruits	Black currant			x			
Fruits	Blackberries			x			
Fruits	Blueberry			x			
Fruits	Cantaloupe			x			
Fruits	Cherry, sour				x		
Fruits	Cherry, sweet			x			
Fruits	Clementines			x			

Fruits	Coconut, fresh				x		
Fruits	Cranberry			x			
Fruits	Currant			x			
Fruits	Dates			x			
Fruits	Dates (dried)			x			
Fruits	Fig juice powder			x			
Fruits	Figs (dried)				x		
Fruits	Figs (raw)				x		
Fruits	Fresh lemon				x		
Fruits	Goji berries			x			
Fruits	Gooseberry, ripe			x			
Fruits	Grapefruit			x			
Fruits	Grapes (ripe)			x			
Fruits	Italian plum			x			
Fruits	Limes				x		
Fruits	Mandarin orange		x				
Fruits	Mango			x			
Fruits	Nectarine			x			
Fruits	Orange			x			
Fruits	Papaya			x			
Fruits	Peach			x			
Fruits	Pear			x			
Fruits	Pineapple		x				
Fruits	Pomegranate		x				
Fruits	Raspberry		x				
Fruits	Red currant			x			
Fruits	Rose hips		x				
Fruits	Strawberries			x			
Fruits	Strawberry			x			
Fruits	Tangerine			x			
Fruits	Tomato					x	
Fruits	Watermelon			x			
Fruits	Yellow plum			x			
Grains & Legumes	Basmati rice			x			
Grains & Legumes	Brown rice		x				
Grains & Legumes	Buckwheat				x		
Grains & Legumes	Bulgar wheat			x			
Grains & Legumes	Couscous			x			
Grains & Legumes	Granulated soy *(cooked, ground)*					x	
Grains & Legumes	kamut				x		

Category	Food	R	O	Y	LG	G	DG
Grains & Legumes	Lentils				x		
Grains & Legumes	Lima beans					x	
Grains & Legumes	Oats			x			
Grains & Legumes	Rye bread			x			
Grains & Legumes	Soy flour				x		
Grains & Legumes	Soy lecithin, pure						x
Grains & Legumes	Soy nuts *(soaked soy beans, then dried)*						x
Grains & Legumes	Soybeans, fresh					x	
Grains & Legumes	Spelt				x		
Grains & Legumes	Tofu				x		
Grains & Legumes	Wheat		x				
Grains & Legumes	white (navy) beans					x	
Meat, Poultry & Fish	Beef	x					
Meat, Poultry & Fish	Boar (wild)		x				
Meat, Poultry & Fish	Chicken		x				
Meat, Poultry & Fish	Duck		x				
Meat, Poultry & Fish	Fresh water fish		x				
Meat, Poultry & Fish	Liver			x			
Meat, Poultry & Fish	Ocean fish		x				
Meat, Poultry & Fish	Offal meats			x			
Meat, Poultry & Fish	Oysters			x			
Meat, Poultry & Fish	Pork	x					
Meat, Poultry & Fish	sardines (canned)	x					
Meat, Poultry & Fish	Tuna (canned)	x					
Meat, Poultry & Fish	Veal	x					
Meat, Poultry & Fish	Wild salmon & some select oily fish				x		
Misc	Apple Cider Vinegar			x			
Misc	Baking soda					x	
Misc	Bee pollen				x		
Misc	Canned foods		x				
Misc	cereals (like Kelloggs etc)		x				
Misc	Hummus			x			
Misc	Microwaved foods	x					
Misc	POPCORN			x			
Misc	Rice milk			x			
Misc	Royal Jelly				x		
Misc	Soy Protein Powder			x			
Misc	Tempeh			x			
Misc	Whey protein powder			x			

Category	Item	R	O	Y	LG	G	DG
Nuts	Almond				x		
Nuts	Almond butter (raw)				x		
Nuts	Brazil nuts			x			
Nuts	Cashews			x			
Nuts	Filberts			x			
Nuts	Hazelnut			x			
Nuts	Macadamia nuts (raw)			x			
Nuts	Peanut butter (raw, organic)		x				
Nuts	Peanuts		x				
Nuts	pine nuts (raw)				x		
Nuts	Pistachios		x				
Nuts	Walnuts				x		
Roots	Carrot				x		
Roots	Fresh red beet					x	
Roots	Kohlrabi				x		
Roots	Potatoes				x		
Roots	Red radish					x	
Roots	Rutabaga				x		
Roots	Summer black radish						x
Roots	sweet potatoes			x			
Roots	Turnip				x		
Roots	White radish (spring)				x		
Roots	Yams				x		
Seeds	Barley				x		
Seeds	Caraway seeds				x		
Seeds	Cumin seeds				x		
Seeds	Fennel seeds				x		
Seeds	Flax seeds			x			
Seeds	Pumpkin seeds			x			
Seeds	Sesame seeds				x		
Seeds	Sunflower seeds			x			
Seeds	Wheat Kernel		x				
Sweets & Sweeteners	Agave nectar			x			
Sweets & Sweeteners	Alcohol sugars		x				
Sweets & Sweeteners	Artificial sweeteners	x					
Sweets & Sweeteners	Barley malt syrup			x			

Sweets & Sweeteners	Beet sugar		x				
Sweets & Sweeteners	Brown rice syrup			x			
Sweets & Sweeteners	Chocolates		x				
Sweets & Sweeteners	Barley malt sweetener			x			
Sweets & Sweeteners	Dried sugar cane juice			x			
Sweets & Sweeteners	Fructose			x			
Sweets & Sweeteners	Halva [ground sesame seed sweet]		x				
Sweets & Sweeteners	Honey			x			
Sweets & Sweeteners	Maple Syrup			x			
Sweets & Sweeteners	Milk sugar			x			
Sweets & Sweeteners	Molasses		x				
Sweets & Sweeteners	Sugar (white)		x				
Sweets & Sweeteners	Sugarcane		x				
Sweets & Sweeteners	Xylitol		x				
Vegetables	Alfalfa					x	
Vegetables	Alfalfa grass						x
Vegetables	Artichokes				x		
Vegetables	Asparagus				x		
Vegetables	Aubergine/Egg plant				x		
Vegetables	Barley grass						x
Vegetables	Basil				x		
Vegetables	Bell peppers/capsicums (all colors)				x		
Vegetables	Blue-Green Algae			x			
Vegetables	Brussels sprouts				x		
Vegetables	Cabbage lettuce, fresh					x	
Vegetables	Canned vegetables		x				

Vegetables	Cauliflower				x		
Vegetables	Cayenne pepper					x	
Vegetables	Celery					x	
Vegetables	Chives				x		
Vegetables	Cilantro					x	
Vegetables	Comfrey				x		
Vegetables	Cooked vegetables (all kinds)			x			
Vegetables	Cucumber, fresh						x
Vegetables	Dandelion						x
Vegetables	Dog grass						x
Vegetables	Endive, fresh					x	
Vegetables	French cut (*green*) beans					x	
Vegetables	Frozen vegetables		x				
Vegetables	Garlic					x	
Vegetables	Ginger					x	
Vegetables	Ginseng				x		
Vegetables	Green cabbage, *(December Harvest)*				x		
Vegetables	Green cabbage, *(March Harvest)*				x		
Vegetables	Horse radish				x		
Vegetables	Kale						x
Vegetables	Kamut grass						x
Vegetables	Lamb's lettuce				x		
Vegetables	Leeks (bulbs)				x		
Vegetables	Lettuce				x		
Vegetables	Mushrooms		x				
Vegetables	Mustard greens				x		
Vegetables	Onion				x		
Vegetables	Oregano					x	
Vegetables	Pak Choy				x		
Vegetables	Parsnips				x		
Vegetables	Peas, fresh				x		
Vegetables	Peas, ripe				x		
Vegetables	Peppers				x		
Vegetables	Pickled vegetables	x					
Vegetables	Pumpkins (raw)				x		
Vegetables	Raw onions				x		
Vegetables	Red cabbage				x		
Vegetables	Rhubarb stalks				x		
Vegetables	Savoy Cabbage				x		

Vegetables	Sea Vegetables				x	
Vegetables	Seaweed (dulse, kelp, laver, etc)				x	
Vegetables	Sorrel					x
Vegetables	Sauerkraut		x			
Vegetables	Soy Sprouts						x
Vegetables	Spinach *(March harvest)*				x	
Vegetables	Spinach *(other than March)*					x
Vegetables	Sprouted seeds (all kinds)						x
Vegetables	Squash (all kinds, raw)				x	
Vegetables	Thyme				x	
Vegetables	Tomatoes (puree)				x	
Vegetables	Tomatoes (raw)				x	
Vegetables	Tomatoes (sundried)				x	
Vegetables	Watercress				x	
Vegetables	Wheat grass						x
Vegetables	White cabbage				x	
Vegetables	Yeast			x		
Vegetables	Zucchini (courgette)				x	

CEASE TO BE OBESE (OR FAT).

Virtually everything you eat has been chemically treated somewhere along the line. Your body, especially when you use processed foods, has to deal with emulsifiers, preservatives, dyes, artificial flavours, humectants, drying agents, bleaches, neutralisers, artificial sweeteners, disinfectants, thickeners, anti-foaming and anti-caking agents, deodorants, alkalisers, extenders, gases, conditioners, hydrogenators, hydrolysers, maturers, sulphites, fumigants, sulphur dioxide, anti-fungal preservatives, stabilisers, texturisers, antibiotics, steroids and irradiation products.

The oft repeated excuse, used by food industry spokesmen (and incredibly believed by the public and the governments), is that because these chemicals are used in such small amounts they are harmless (in spite of the fact that they cause cancer in experimental animals). Some of these chemicals are so poisonous that they would kill humans instantly if eaten in quantity and the frightening truth is that even tiny amounts of these often carcinogenic substances are enough to cause severe problems and often cancer in susceptible individuals.

The director of the US Food and Drug Administration Toxicological Division has said that there is no precise understanding of the ultimate fate of food additives once they're in the body. In fact, years ago it was thought that the body was able to detoxify food additives and that they were broken down into harmless compounds. It's now known that this doesn't happen.

What does happen, however, is that your body shunts this poisonous cocktail into its storage mode as fat.

This fat then builds up a toxic load containing benzyl alcohol, isopropyl alcohol, ethyl alcohol, propylene glycol, glycerine mannitol, sorbitol, polydextrose, ethyl acetate, glyceryl monoacetate, glycerol diacetate, triacetin, triethyl citrate, edible fats and oils, sodium chloride, erythritol, modifying agents, natural starches, maltodextrin, gelatine, hydrogenated oils, calcium silicide, potassium caseinate, sodium aluminosilicate, magnesium carbonate, calcium phosphate, tribasic and calcium hydroxyphosphate.

There is much truth in the saying, "the whiter the bread, the sooner you're dead.

The bottom line here is that if you want to avoid becoming overweight and if you want to stay healthy, you cannot afford to eat processed food!

OBESITY.

Obesity is caused by an excess of fructose to which a high proportion of us have now become addicted. Sugar is highly addictive and since almost everybody in the developed industrialised world consumes about 130 pounds of it a year, the net result is an obesity epidemic which brings with it heart disease, diabetes, and a dramatic shortening of life.

The Answer.

Paleo-biologists have performed DNA footprint analysis of 10,000 year old stool samples from caves in Texas. These have allowed them to determine that our ancestors ate about 100 grams of fibre a day (our consumption is currently 12 grams).

Dietary fibre found in fruits, vegetables, whole grains and legumes is the part of the plant that the human is unable to digest. There are two types of fibre:-

Soluble, which dissolves in water and insoluble which doesn't. The difference determines each type of fibres impact on your body, health and stool. Soluble fibre slows digestion and absorption and is fermented by the bacteria of your colon into gases. Insoluble fibre on the other hand, consists of polysaccharides (non-glucose carbohydrates) such as cellulose which is the stringy stuff in celery. They're not digested at all.

Used in our metabolism the two together are an unbeatable pair. The insoluble fibre forms a lattice work for the soluble fibre to sit on whilst the soluble fibre bridges the gaps in the lattice work to maintain its integrity. By inhibiting the rate of flux from the intestine crossing into the bloodstream, fibre gives the liver a chance to fully metabolise what's coming in so there's no overflow.

Once fibre is consumed with a meal it forms a gelatinous barrier between the food and the intestinal wall. This delays the intestine's ability to absorb glucose, fructose and fat. By slowing down glucose absorption, the blood-glucose rise is attenuated which limits the peak glucose. In return, the pancreas, sensing the slower and lower rise in blood glucose, limits its response and reduces the amount of insulin released. Less insulin means less shunting of energy to fat thereby reducing the total load on the body. The way to both satisfy your craving for sweet things and to get much needed fibre into your diet is to consume ripe fruit. In ripe fruit, fructose is, for the most part, mitigated by the presence of fibre and since soluble fibre forms a sticky gel delaying the emptying of your stomach, you feel full faster.

Accordingly, higher dietary fibre limits the total food intake and because fibre delivers more nutrients further down the intestine where the bacteria can utilise them for energy, fibre then helps to keep the beneficial bacterial balance in your digestive system.

Exercise.

If you want to lose weight, exercise is the single best thing you can do for yourself and a recent study in Taiwan looking at the death rates of over 400,000 subjects shows that moderate intensity exercise for 15 minutes a day can increase lifespan by as much as three years (even in patients with known heart disease).

Recent studies have demonstrated that fitness mitigates all the negative effects of obesity on visceral fat, health complaints and longevity.

So irrespective of weight, consistent exercise (even just 15 minutes a day) is a single best way for people to improve their health. That's 273 hours paid in for three years of life gained or a 64,000 per cent return on an investment!

Still hungry!

There is a huge difference between the phenomenon of satiety versus the phenomenon of lack of hunger. The signal for satiety is peptide yy. Between the stomach and the pyy cells are 22 feet of intestine. It takes time for the food to get there, so give it a chance. The key is to wait 20 minutes after you've eaten the first portion and in that time you'll really know whether you want to eat any more. The best way to get your pyy fully operational is to make the food move through the intestine faster and that's the job of fibre. The best way to get fibre is to eat real food!

Always eat breakfast and always eat protein at breakfast because it has a higher thermic effect meaning it costs double the energy to metabolise protein versus carbohydrates.

Do not eat after 7 o'clock in the evening because any energy consumed that late will have no chance to be burned. It will find its way either to the fat tissue or to the liver and in either case can interfere with your sleep and general well being.

Proteins versus carbohydrates.

Follow the example set by millions of years of experience of our ancestors and eat only one of the two above at a time. If you're going to eat protein, then just eat protein, do not mix it with carbohydrate. Or if you're going to eat carbohydrate, just eat carbohydrate and do not mix it with protein. This is an enormous benefit to your liver which, provided that you don't over eat, will have much less work to do since only one of its digestive pathways will be working at that time. Our ancestors did not have access to fish and chips, nor to meat and two veg. They either had the meat or the two veg! This is how our digestive system is meant to operate and this is how it's developed over millions of years.

So finally:-

Avoid sugar in all its forms. It is dangerous, addictive, makes you fat and kills you younger.

Next, exercise for 15 minutes each day. This might sound impossible if you're a very busy person but it will add years to your life. By simply walking, you do a lot of good. The reason for this is that the veins on the bottom of your feet are structured in such a way as to flatten as your weight transfers on to them and this has the effect of forcing the blood back up the leg, it being held in check and prevented from falling back by a series of valve-like structures in the veins in your legs. This walking foot pump is vital to your health and dramatically improves the circulation of your life giving blood.

Fast or go without one meal a day or cut down the size of your meals to the point where you always get up from the table slightly hungry. The Japanese have a very wise saying which is, eat until you are 80% full.

Your stomach is not a rubbish bin and everything you put into it affects your health.

Eat fibrous food. Satisfy your cravings for sweetness with ripe fruit, preferably uncooked. Eat lots of fibrous salads and vegetables, first making sure that they're fresh and organically grown. (If you're in any way uncertain about this go back and read the section on pesticides in foods and decide whether you want to kill yourself by building up a toxic load of chemicals or whether you want to live healthy and longer).

Drink lots of water, more illness is caused by dehydration than any other single factor and copious amounts of water help flush out toxins from your system and keep it operating optimally.

Learn to prepare your own food using organically grown ingredients. All processed food is chock full of preservatives and has been produced more or less industrially using a host of chemicals that you don't want to eat!

Finally, try to secure a supply of fresh unpolluted food.

Fresh food.

Fresh means picked no more than a few hours ago, which you will almost never find in a High Street shop or supermarket.

Fruit and vegetables begin to lose their nutrients the moment they are picked. Not only do storage conditions like heat and humidity deplete the vitamins and, to a lesser extent, the minerals they've absorbed from the earth, but the plants continue to breath in oxygen for a few days which speeds the rotting process. Meantime, enzymes in the plants consume the nutrients in a hopeless attempt to survive so that all food, particularly vegetables has a "half life".

Suppose a leaf vegetable has a half life of 48 hours. Two days after picking, only 50% of the original nutrition remains. Two more days later, half of the remaining half has gone, leaving only 25% and two further days, half the 25% has been lost. Thus six days after picking a leaf vegetable contains only an eighth of its original nutrition.

More sturdy fruit and root vegetables and hard fruits, like apples, have a slower nutrition erosion wait, but since all fruit in supermarkets and indeed all food in supermarkets is at least seven days old, then sourcing of fresh food is quite a problem in this civilisation.

However, it's well worthwhile spending time setting up arrangements with a range of local growers so as to make sure that the food on your plate contains the maximum amount of nutrients.

Conclusion.

As a dietary and anti-obesity guide, try putting yourself in the place of our hunter-gatherer forebears. Way back then our people ate frugally of whatever was available, carbohydrates at one time, and protein at another. They exercised, walking substantial distances each day in bare feet or skin moccasins. They sang, danced, painted, squatted round a fire, swam, studied the stars at night, indulged in occasional bursts of exercise running away from predators and/or hunting. They were rarely still, drank mostly water, searched for and ate sweet fruit that was very ripe and had the occasional honey treat perhaps once a year.

This is how human beings evolved and were meant to live and this is the mindset you should adopt when seeking to lose weight and live longer.

SOY – HEALTH FOOD?

The properties of soy are promoted by nutritionists, doctors, popular health and beauty publications, all of whom are ignorant of the scientific facts. There is a
very hazardous side to soy that we need to know about.

For example, the article *Soya Bean Goitre*, report three cases. The New England Journal of Medicine 1960 262 (22:1099-1103) lays out three cases of infants developing goitre when they were fed soya bean formula. The condition was rapidly eliminated in two of the infants when the soy formula was withdrawn. The third child was cured when iodine was added to the diet.

What did soya formula have to do with thyroid (goitre) problems? Well soya beans are a source of isoflavonoids, including genistein and daidzein. Contrary to what is often reported in the media, they're both hazardous to your health. In 1997 an article in Bio-Chemical Pharmacology No. 52:1087-1096; "soya beans contain compounds (genistein and daidzein – the active ingredients), that inhibit the action of the thyroid peroxidase (TPO) which is essential to thyroid hormone synthesis".

So soya beans are not good for the thyroid!

The popular phyto-oestrogens genistein and daidzein are actually endocrine destructors. Women around the world have been misled.

In fact soy contains phytates which "magnetise out" essential nutrients like iodine.

The murder conviction in Atlanta, USA, of some vegan parents whose six week baby died of starvation underscores the dangers of vegan ideology to infants. To supplement the mother's inadequate supply of breast milk, the parents had fed their son soya milk and apple juice. The baby was only 3.5 1bs when he died of starvation in April 2004.

According to K.T. Daniel PhD, author of The Whole Soya Story (the dark side of
America's favourite food), soya milk should never be given to infants in place of formula.

In 1990 the Food and Drug Administration issued a warning about the use of soya milk for infants stating that it is grossly lacking in the nutrients needed for infants, and asked all manufacturers to put warning labels on soya milk so it would not be used as formula substitutes.

The myth that soy is a health food has led many parents, particularly vegans, who use no animal products, to believe that soya milk is a complete and nourishing food, not only for adults but for babies and children. The reverse is true and severe vitamin, mineral, fatty acid and amino acid deficiencies will occur when it's used wrongly in this way. That's why supplements are required by law to be added to soy infant formula.

In 2003, the deaths of three Israeli infants from improperly manufactured soy formula led the Israeli Health Ministry to form a 30 member committee of paediatricians, oncologists and toxicologists to investigate soy formula and soy foods. In July 2005 the Ministry issued a health advisory warning that babies should not receive soy formula (except as a last resort) and that children up to 18 should not eat soya foods or drink soya milk more than once a day to a maximum of three times a week.

The Ministry was concerned about many health issues, including adverse effects on fertility and increased cancer risk.

The governments of the UK, Switzerland and New Zealand have also warned that the soya infant formula should only be used as a last resort and soya milk should never be used at all.

Today the United States Food and Drug Administration, Department of Health and Human Services, list 288 records of soy at its "FDA poisonous plant database" (March 2006 revision). Their website will shock you since it reveals that soy is anything but a health food.

Soy harms your immune system too. Back in 1975 the Canadian Journal of Biochemistry reported that soya beans actually weaken your immune system. "Soya bean trypsin inhibitor was found to inhibit the transformation of human lymphocytes etc."

Here's why this happens:-
Trypsin is an enzyme produced by your pancreas and used in digesting proteins; it is critical for antibody production. An inhibitor is something that disables so you can think of this as rather like having one foot on the accelerator of your car and the other on the brake at the same time.

So a trypsin inhibitor will irritate your pancreas, stressing it to produce hormones when it can't, leading to decreased oxygenation from the irritation. Soy prevents the protein you eat from being fully utilised and digested. Your immune system then can't get fuel with proper antibodies and lymphocytes and therefore soy is cancer causing in your pancreas, and cancer of the pancreas is typically a death sentence.

Because of bad advice, many women, especially, have decreased amounts of animal based protein they consume in favour of soy. You should resist this incorrect activity and minimise your chances of contracting both thyroid and pancreatic cancer accordingly. There are many non-animal and non-soy protein available as healthy alternatives (e.g. nuts, legumes, pulses etc).

Soya is intended in nature as an animal food to be grazed by cattle which have five stomachs in which to process it, as opposed to the one stomach that we have. We simply cannot process soya effectively and it leads inevitably to pancreatic exhaustion, a major contributory factor in both cancer and diabetes Type 2.

Cheap to produce and nasty in use, soya is __not__ a health food!

NON-HUMAN INTELLIGENCE!

According to 2007 national institutes of health estimate, 90% of cells in the human body are bacterial, fungal or otherwise non-human. Although many have concluded that bacteria enjoy a commensal relationship with their human hosts, only a fraction of the human micro-biota has been characterised, much less identified.

The sheer number of non-human genes represented by the human micro-biota implies that we have just begun to fathom the full extent to which bacteria work to facilitate their own survival.

A healthy human adult harbours some one hundred trillion bacteria in the gut alone. This is ten times as many bacterial cells as the individual has cells descended from the sperm and egg or his or her parents. These bugs, are diverse. Egg and sperm provide about 23,000 different genes. Whereas, the micro-biome, as the body's commensal bacteria are collectively known, is reckoned to have around 3 million.

A useful way to think of the micro-biome is as an additional human organ. It weighs as much as many organs (about a kilogram, or a bit more than 2 pounds). Although it is not a distinct structure in the way that the heart or liver is distinct, an organ doesn't have to have form and shape to be real. For example, the immune system consists of cells scattered all around the body but it has the salient feature of an organ, namely that it is an organised system of cells.

Self-preservation.

It was once thought that we are what we eat, but to be more accurate we are what digests and assimilates our food! It all has to do with a thriving population of 100 trillion life-promoting bacteria; that take up residence within our digestive tract from the moment of birth. These are a diverse group numbering between 500 to 1,000 different species and in a healthy person these bacteria live in a balanced eco system with each species inhabiting its appropriate place.

However, since the introduction of antibiotics, steroids, birth control pills and a radical alteration in our diet, this balance has been disturbed. For example, there is a distinctive change in the inter-intestinal microbial populations found in obese humans and lean humans. They have different microbes in their gut which indicates that there is a strong connection between what we eat, how much we eat, and the species of bacteria that inhabit the intestinal tract. Clearly then your food choices have an instantaneous effect on the balance of gut flora as this flexes to accommodate its primal urge which is to survive.

The shape changers.

The scientific community has adopted the concept of mono-morphism based on the work of Louis Pasteur in the late 19th century. This concept means that microbes always maintain their basic shape as virus, bacterium or fungus. As we shall see, this concept is badly flawed, indeed wrong.

Pleomorphism as coined by the French chemist and biologist Antoine Béchamp, refers to the ability of microbes to change from one form to another like a caterpillar changing into a butterfly and it was a German professor of zoology and microbiology, Günther Enderlein, who in 1925 described the different stages of a microbe that is normally present in the blood as tiny colloidal protein units. The Enderlein structures he observed grow into increasingly higher bacterial forms and finally into fungi. This process depends upon the acid/alkaline balance in the stomach and therefore in the blood and several other researchers including Royal Raymond Rife, Wilhelm Reich, Virginia Livingston-Wheeler, Alan Cantwell and Gaston Naessens have described the same phenomena.

The truth about germs.

"There is only one physiological disease – the over acidification of the body, due primarily to an inverted way of eating and living. This over-acidification leads to the one sickness, or primary symptom which is the overgrowth in the body of micro-organisms, whose poisons produce the symptoms we call "disease" (Dr. Robert O. Young).

In the late 19th century, the brilliant French scientist Antoine Béchamp (1816 – 1908) discovered and scientifically proved the function of, minute indestructible living entities called microzymas which he showed, are the foundation of all life on earth.

Béchamp was able to demonstrate that microzymas exist in every cell and all the bodily fluids and have an innate intelligence that communicates genetic information to the cell. The control signals that microzymas transmit are mediated by the cellular terrain which is another way of saying by the level of acidity or alkalinity in the body.

Microzymas are immortal in the sense that they cannot be destroyed by extreme heat, radiation or any other method that we know of, but because of their functions in controlling the behaviour of cells, they cause cells to change their form, in other words to be pleomorphic.

This means that germs, which are cellular micro-organisms, change their identity according to the cellular terrain/the degree of acidity of the body.

Antoine Béchamp was able to show scientifically that it isn't the bacteria or virus themselves that produce disease but that they are the aftermath of diseased tissue. Disease-associated micro-organisms, the disease condition themselves, that are the result of varying degrees of morbidity/acidity in a low-oxygen, cellular environment created by toxic diet, toxic lifestyle, toxic environmental exposure and toxic emotions (hormonal shifts).

These research findings which have been proven time and again by cellular terrain specialists up to the present time, make a complete nonsense of Louis Pasteur's germ theory of monomorphism where each separate disease is supposedly caused by a separate or specific bacteria or virus.

In his book "The Dream and Lie of Louis Pasteur", Dr. M. L. Leverson, MD, PhD, MA, says "The entire fabric of the germ theory rests upon assumptions which not only have not been proved, but which are incapable of proof, and many of them can be proved to be the reverse of truth! The basic one of these unproved assumptions, the credit for which in its present form is wholly due to Pasteur, is the hypothesis that all the so-called infections and contagious disorders are caused by germs, each disease having is own specific germ, which germs have existed in the air from the beginning of things, and that though the body is closed to pathogenic germs when in good health, when the vitality is lowered the body becomes susceptible to their inroads."

Not much profit in prevention.

The fact that Louis Pasteur had lots of friends in high places who saw profit in the treatment and management of disease, caused his work on germ theory to be preferred over the potentially unprofitable work of Antoine Béchamp and Claude Bernard. Thus, we now have a global medical and pharmaceutical industry doing its best to find "cures" for diseases supposedly caused by germs when in reality germs are the result of pre-existing conditions in the patient's body.

Even Pasteur himself cried out on his death bed, that Claude Bernard, the leading cellular physiologist, was right on target. That is, the germs are nothing, and the cellular terrain is everything!

The true mechanism of disease.

An over-acidic, cellular terrain causes or allows the overgrowth of micro-organisms which are normally kept in balance by healthy pH levels.

When this imbalance happens, it supports the conditions in which the microzymas signals the pleomorphic changes of the overgrowth, germs to bacteria, bacteria to virus, virus to fungal forms and fungal forms to cancer cells. All amply documented, not only in Béchamp and Bernard's work, but also in the work of Otto Warburg, the Nobel Prize winner and more recently in the work of Italian oncologist Dr. Simoncini.

<u>Coughs and sneezes don't cause diseases but they can spread them.</u>

For example, if four people go into a lift and one of them is sneezing and coughing with a cold, then it's quite probable that one of the remaining three will get a cold soon after. He has "caught" an infection from the person with a cold.

But how is it that the other two people don't catch cold when they too were exposed to the sneezes and coughs?

The answer is simple:-

The person who caught the cold was suffering from a reduced immune response because of a reduction in oxygen levels leading to over-acidity in one or other of his systems.

The incoming bacterial or viral load from the origin of the cold simply overloaded his system, which was already pretty run down and this overload expressed itself as a cold.

The other two who had no such problem, the germs couldn't "take" so that no illness resulted.

Acidic pH is the PRIMARY FACTOR in disease and whilst various routes of medication may treat the symptoms, no healing will take place until the body's pH level is returned to normal.

Respiration.

Oxygen has a net negative charge and thus a healthy body depends on a high level of negative electromagnetic charge on cells surfaces for cellular respiration to take place.

Acidity is a positively charged state, so that cellular respiration falls in an acidic environment and the microzymas begin to direct the affected cells to shut down, to die and become toxins.

When someone coughs or sneezes on you and your bloodstream is already in this pre-toxic state, then it doesn't take much to "throw the switch" and push your system into ill-health.

The body will always try to heal itself by expelling toxins via respiration, by expelling germs through coughs and sneezes and by diarrhoea and vomiting.

Looked at in this light, catching a cold may be a good thing in the long run as it can bring you up short and make you realise that you've got a problem!

If you continue in your present mode you could get really ill, so best do something about it now before it's too late, before it dramatically shortens your lifespan.

FOOD AND FOLLY.

The hunters.

During the period of our evolution when we drifted up and down the earth in its various seasons, there were hunters and there were gatherers. Most hunters killed their food while some fished. They ate fat and protein, went long stretches between kills, and had to live off their fat stores. Their livers processed dietary fat in two ways which depended on the hunter's body weight and their current energy supply. If energy was in short supply, their livers would systematically break the fatty acids down into ketones. Fragments of these could then be burnt for energy either by the mitochondria (the portion of the cell where energy generation takes place) in the liver, or in other organs.

If the energy supply was in excess, the liver would package the fat into particles known as low-density lipo-proteins. These particles would circulate in the bloodstream to take up residence in fat cells as triglycerides (blobs of fat stored for another day) when energy might be needed when food was scarce.

Insulin production falls off dramatically with starvation and these stored triglycerides would then break down into free fatty acids when the cycle would complete itself releasing triglycerides into the bloodstream to re-enter the liver and be processed into ketones again. Our bodies were, and are, perfectly adapted to burning fat as an energy source.

The gatherers.

The gatherers derive their food from what grew out of the earth. They ate carbohydrates and proteins in the form of fruits and vegetables. If energy was in short supply, glucose would be taken up by the liver. If energy was in good supply, the liver would not capture some of the glucose and a rise in blood glucose and subsequent insulin release would occur.

If the energy was in great supply, then the blood glucose would rise even higher and insulin would keep pace. This drives energy into fat storage for a rainy day, for example, a famine.

The Omnivore.

In evolutionary terms, the metabolism of fat and carbohydrates developed separately but both metabolic products of these two completely different pathways (fat broken down serially versus carbohydrates undergoing glycosis) arrive at the mitochondria in the form of the compound acetyl-CoA, or ketones. The health of the cell and indeed all cells has everything to do with how much energy the mitochondria have to process at any given time.

The hunters ate fat and their liver would process what it needed for the mitochondrial production of energy and then export any excess as low density lipoprotein to be taken up in the adipose tissue.

The gatherers ate carbohydrates (glucose); their liver would extract what it needed and the insulin would clear the rest out into the bloodstream for muscle and adipose tissue. Any excess glucose would be converted in the liver to glycogen for storage.

Our ancestors were not exclusively hunters or gatherers. They favoured one type of food or another depending on the time of year and where they lived. The liver thus developed two separate pop-off valves to protect it from excess energy throughput, one for carbohydrates and one for fat. In both cases the mitochondrias exposure to ketones was regulated so as not to overwhelm their capacity.

The turning point.

However, about 75,000 years ago we learnt to irrigate and farm and became omnivores. Our entire society began then to eat fat and carbohydrates and as food became more plentiful, we began to overload both sides of our metabolic pathways the E2-carbon breakdown of fat and the glycolysis of carbohydrates. This forces the mitochondria into overdrive when they have to deal with the onslaught of ketones coming from both directions. One high-fat, high-carbohydrate meal is no big deal. But keep this up for 10,000 meals in a row (about ten years) and we're talking about real damage; an increase in chronic metabolic disease or metabolic syndrome.

The natural balance.

With few exceptions, most naturally occurring food stuffs contains either fat or carbohydrates but usually not both. Meat fish and poultry have no carbohydrates. Grains, roots and tubers, for example, potatoes and yams, have no fat. Those fruits that have fat, such as avocados, coconuts and olives, have minimal carbohydrates. Nuts are an exception but they are still low in carbohydrates and high in fibre. Milk is another exception, but other than that, which come from their mothers, humans were not exposed to other mammals milk until the beginnings of agriculture in the neolithic period.

It wasn't until we began eating fat and carbohydrates in the same meal, that our cells first felt the wrath of mitochondrial wear and tear. Indeed, the advent of trade in the early 17th century signal the first outbreaks of the various diseases to which we are now prone. Before that, food was a function of what we killed or grew ourselves.

Our hunter-gatherer forbears who lived on the earth for millions of years in balanced good health, ate one type of food at a time – that which was available. Hunting is a hazardous business with spears, bows and arrows, snares and traps and there's ample evidence to show that many of our neolithc forbears were badly injured in the process. Accordingly, meat eating was a relatively rare experience swinging between feast and famine which allowed our ancestors long periods of time during which to use up the energy stored in their adipose fat layers and bloodstream.

Similarly, tribes moving from place to place would harvest fruits, berries, nuts, grains, tubers and etc. in the course of their migrations. Moving on only when they had eaten out the available resources in a given area.

Accordingly, their diet at one time would be predominantly nuts, another time predominantly berries, another time predominantly fruit and so forth.

To eat the two food sources together was rare as a consequence of which our ancestors were superbly healthy (the Palaeolithic was probably the time when we were most healthy as skeletal remains have shown) and lived much longer than we do now.

The ideal human diet then for longevity is very rare meals of protein interspersed with very long periods when you only eat carbohydrates. Never the two together.

Folly.

Overloading on food has put an enormous strain on our metabolism resulting in a plethora of diseases and, more to the point for our purposes, in an epidemic of obesity. We're thirty years into an obesity pandemic and it's getting progressively worse and the reason for this is sugar.

Nutritionists routinely categorise sugar as empty calories, so interchangeable with calories from starch. But sugar has a special pay load. It's made up of half glucose and half fructose. The fructose makes it sweet and that ultimately is the molecule we seek.

So sugar, despite being a carbohydrate, is really both a fat (because that's how fructose is metabolised in the liver) and a carbohydrate because that's how glucose is metabolised) all rolled into one. Both pathways have to work overtime which is why sugar is the real omnivores dilemma.

Sugar is addictive to humans and has an opiate-like effect with its ability to reduce pain and cause withdrawal symptoms.

It's also habitually addictive since we are hard-wired in our brains to seek out sweeteners.

Evolutionarily, sweeteners were the signal to our ancestors that something was safe to eat. This is because no sweet foods are acutely poisonous.

Thus, we gravitate to sweeteners as a default. For example, to introduce new food to a baby, you have to offer it about ten to thirteen times. But if that new food is sweet, you only have to offer it once. Accordingly when we are reaching for some sweet, processed food to eat, we're simply obeying an evolutionary imperative which is designed to drive us toward sweet ripe fruit.

In the modern diet, fructose has increased both as a percentage of our caloric intake and our total consumption. We currently consume sugar at a rate of about 6.5 ounces a day or 130 pounds a year. Our current consumption has increased five-fold compared to a 100 years ago and more than doubled in the last 30 years. Plus it's added to food when it's processed so that the inescapable reality is that 20 to 25% of all the calories we consume, a total of 22 teaspoons per day, comes from some variation of sugar.

All caloric sweeteners contain fructose; white sugar, cane sugar, beet sugar, fruit sugar, table sugar, brown sugar, maple syrup, honey and agave nectar. It's all the same. The carrier is irrelevant. It's what it contains that matters. Sugar consumption is a big problem. 33% of sugar consumption comes from beverages and 1.4 billion people today are obese and the figure is rising exponentially.

The Max Planck Institute in Germany has shown experimentally that sugar attacks the collagen bonds in our skin, separating them from the fibroblast cells which make them. Therefore, sugar reduces skin elasticity and accelerates ageing.

On a population level, the fatter you are, the quicker you die and it's your waist circumference which correlates with morbidity and risk for death better than any other health parameter!

Worldwide, more than 1.4 billion people are overweight, whereas only 800 million are underweight and these statistics are diverging rapidly. Moreover, there are serious consequences to being overweight which can radically change the cause of a person's life. Fat is toxic and potentially lethal! Just carrying as few as an extra 4.5 kilos (10 pounds) over your ideal weight is considered a serious risk factor for heart disease, diabetes, high blood pressure, dementia, Alzheimer's disease, liver disease, hormonal imbalances, depression and cancer. In fact at least 30 different diseases are related to being overweight and this number too is proliferating.

The brain.

Overwhelming evidence now reveals that your expanding waistline could put a serious crimp on your brain size as well as your brain power.

Researchers set out to discover if being overweight posed a serious danger to the brain and scanned the brains of 94 people over the age of 70. The results were quite shocking. Overweight people had 4% less brain tissue than people of normal weight. For obese people the findings were even worse. They had 8% less brain tissue than people of normal weight. The study showed that carrying extra weight not only degenerated the brain, but also accelerated its ageing.

Researcher, Paul Thompson, showed his observation "the brains of overweight people looked eight years older than the brains of those who were lean and 16 years older in obese people. Type-2 diabetes, which is common in the overweight, is known to accelerate the ageing of the brain and the onset of dementia.

Vitamin D.

Vitamin D is really a steroid hormone rather than an actual vitamin. Known as the sunshine vitamin, it is in fact proven to be protective against 13 different types of cancer and optimal Vitamin D levels are critical for good health.

Increased fatty cells can decrease the ability to make Vitamin D by a factor of 4 and Vitamin D is also a factor linked to an increased risk of developing Type-2 diabetes. Low levels of Vitamin D are also known to nearly double the risk of cardiovascular disease and people deficient in Vitamin D tend to have a higher risk of heart attack and stroke.

Conversely, high levels of Vitamin D increase your ability to lose weight and losing weight will increase your Vitamin D levels – all of which will reduce your risk of metabolic syndrome, insulin resistance, diabetes and cardiovascular disease, not to mention most chronic illnesses.

<u>Sleep</u>.

An expanding body of scientific evidence shows that the less sleep you get, the more cravings you have, the more calories you eat, the more belly fat you have and the higher your body mass index. Sleep-deprived people eat more carbohydrates than the well rested and people with less than four hours sleep are proven to choose sweets, cakes and biscuits over fruit, vegetables and dairy products.

Since the physiological manifestations of fatigue, sleep and hunger are similar, people sometimes confuse them. That's why people tend to eat when they're really feeling tired. Fatigue is often misinterpreted as hunger.

As we've seen earlier, there's a strong connection between what we eat and how much we eat, and the species of bacteria that inhabit the intestinal tract. Junk food diets rich in sugar alter healthy gut flora resulting in more obese tendencies. Thus your food choices have an instantaneous effect on your balance of gut flora.

Conclusion.

Maintaining a healthy brain, ensuring optimal Vitamin D levels, committing to regenerative sleep and supporting the growth of healthy intestinal flora are some of the factors involved in recovering from a world drowning in fat. But the main arbiter of obesity is sugar. Sugar in all its form is used in every kind of processed food and, since as we've seen our brains are wired for reward, its use is obsessive.

Sugar, in all its forms, is the main culprit in the accelerated ageing we're seeing around us and as a strong oxygen grabber, makes the proteins in and between our cells stick together (cross linking) reducing the available oxygen in our bodies and causing them to acidify.

SLEEP DEPRIVATION.

Having too little sleep negatively affects energy, memory, learning, thinking, alertness, productivity, creativity, safety, health, quality of life and longevity. It also makes you fat!

The reason that lack of sleep makes you fat is that sleep deprivation lowers levels of the hormone leptin, an absence of which triggers the overconsumption of carbohydrates. Anyone who's had a bad night's sleep will be familiar with cravings for toast, cereal and croissants.

Secondly, lack of sleep can cause levels of growth hormones to plummet by 75%. These repair hormones are secreted during the deep stage of sleep and help maintain the proportion of muscle to fat in the body. Too little growth hormone increases our fat stores.

Blood sugar is also adversely affected, since having less than 7 hours sleep causes it to shoot up after breakfast and remain at double the usual level throughout the morning. In turn, this triggers extra insulin which stimulates hunger and fat storage.

Thirdly, lack of sleep also increases afternoon levels of cortisol, another appetite stimulating hormone, which, once again, stimulates our hunger mechanism.

The loss of even an hour of sleep for two or three nights in a row results in increased levels of the hormone cortisol and decreases in growth hormones and prolactin, the opposite of changing that should occur during sleep. Another change involves the reduced production of the energy-carrier molecule, adenosine triphosphate (ATP). A bad night's sleep results in an inadequate supply of ATP for the next day and an excess of the fatigue signalling chemical adenosine.

Long-term sleep deprivation (less than 7 to 10 hours a night for ten years) carries severe health warnings including increased risk of heart disease, higher fat storage, an impaired immune system, possible harm to brain cells, faster ageing, memory impairment and depression.

How does lack of sleep affect the memory? It's simple! When we first go to sleep we fall into a very deep sleep during which time the body does all its housekeeping and repair work.

During later sleep we go through a period of REM sleep (rapid eye movement sleep) and it's during this time, during this period of REM sleep, that the previous day's experiences are transferred to long-term memory via a mechanism known as the "sleep spindle". The "sleep spindle" is a series of one or two second bursts of very high frequency brain waves. This is used to transport memories in the form of neural patterns to the hippocampus, and resupplies our system with brain chemicals used up the previous day. Without REM sleep and this spindling process, memories dissipate, we become absent minded and lose focus.

During REM sleep and to facilitate the distribution within our system of brain chemicals used up the previous day, we normally experience muscle paralysis. This comes in short bursts in conjunction with the sleep spindle and acts as superb marker for future memory disorders.

According to Dr. Melissa Murray, a neuro-scientist at Mayo Clinic in Florida:-

Screening for the sleep disorder wherein people act out dreams while asleep (here she quotes a disorder involving, for example, holding a steering wheel whilst dreaming about driving a car) can be a very good indicator of a predisposition to dementia with Lewy bodies. This is a form of dementia difficult to distinguish from Alzheimers but as many as 75 to 80% of men with dementia with Lewy bodies do experience REM sleep behaviour disorders.

According to ACS chemical neuro-science, the journal of the American chemical society, a Mediterranean diet high in virgin olive oil helps destroy proteins that cause Alzheimers and by default we're again back to the proposition that it's only by eating an aberrant diet (high in trans fats and the like) that we subject ourselves to the possibility of Parkinsons, Alzheimers and etc in old age.

At least 8 hours sleep per night on a regular basis is vital to good health, to weight loss and to longevity.

MAGNETISM AND EARTHING.

The human body is made up of up to 90% water. This water has a high saline content which makes it a very good conductor of electricity and the cerebro-spinal fluid is made up of almost pure Vitamin C which is an extraordinarily good conductor of electrons. Finally, the brain is made up of totally unsaturated fatty proteins so that it behaves as an organic, body-temperature super conductor. There being no resistance to the passage of electromagnetic currents through its medium.

The whole structure of our bodies and particularly the brain-spine complex act as a perfect biological antenna conducting fluctuations in the earth's electromagnetic field throughout the entire structure. These fluctuations have a major effect on our hormones and as far back as 1964 L. Gross showed that a small difference in a magnetic field can produce physical effects:-

Magnetic fields modify the way functions of electrons in macro-molecules, producing a greater paramagnetic susceptibility, which leads to a slow down in reaction speed and the rate at which the RNA and DNA are synthesised.

In other words, the replication of DNA macro-molecules is mediated by the action of the fluctuation in the earth's magnetic field. DNA is very sensitive to magnetic fields and turns perpendicularly to a magnetic field. Its electromagnetic sympathy is implicit in its structure and behaviour since it's a left-handed spiral form.

The earth's magnetic field has fluctuated over the millennia and these fluctuations have had a profound effect on humankind, particularly on our life span.

Dr. Okai of Kyorin University in Japan has discovered an increase in the life span of red blood cells in the bodies of mice and a strong magnetic field environment. Human beings are not mice but our metabolisms are very similar and Dr. Okai hypothesises that the substantial increase in longevity in his test subjects may be due to the sterilising action and other positive life prolonging attributes possessed by the magnetic field.

Magnetic fields on health.

Any conducting substance moving in the presence of a magnetic field generates electricity. Accordingly, the blood flow generates electricity which ionises the blood and as we're seeing when any molecule is ionised, it's very active. Accordingly, the magnetic field and your heart pumping energy force the separation of plus and minus ions and these active ions have been detected to loosen and chip away plaque and cholesterol build up in the arteries.

In its active stage, each ion has an electric field which induces water to be hexagonally structured and active. Consequently, the water content of the blood is extremely sensitive to fluctuations in the earth's magnetic field and throughout the billions of years of our evolution, it's axiomatic that our life expectancy has fluctuated in direct proportion to the strength of the earth's magnetic field.

Decline.

The earth's magnetic field has been measurably declining for the last 300 years and it is postulated by many leading scientists that we are now entering a period of time when the earth's polarity will reverse. This has happened many times throughout history and is usually a time of much chaos, strife, ill-health and systemic collapse.

At this point, it's worth the mention that on a personal level, you can strengthen your own exposure to the earth's magnetic field by wearing a small array of magnets.

These significantly improve your circulation and the quality of your blood in ionic terms as well as boosting the hormonal activity within your structure.

The wearing of a properly constructed magnetic device actually strengthens the electrical currents in your body. This is because any electrolyte (such as human blood) moving through a magnetic field will have a strengthened electrical potential.

By properly constructed, I mean that the device must be negative toward the body and positive away, since the flow of magnetic gauss is from positive to negative. In this way we put energy into the flow rather than taking it out.

Diurnal flow.

As it circles the earth the moon "pumps" the ionosphere up and down as it pulls the tides around the planet. This has the effect of pumping the energy flow of electrons from the negative earth to the positive ionosphere and this pumping action causes the electrons to flow along the metabolic pathways of the body which are the energy lines of classical acupuncture.

Using an electron microscope, one can actually see electrons entering and exiting the skin at acupuncture points where they form a helical flow which helix or vortex directs the pressure of the electronic flow in and out of the body. This is known in Chinese medicine as the flow of "chi" or "prana" in the Hindu tradition. Human beings, and indeed all living creatures, are subjected to this energy flow and have a magnetic sensitivity which in man is centred on the pineal gland (the third eye) which sensitivity in large part affects the electromagnetic activity in their bodies. By insulating oneself from this flow of energy, one is shortening one's life and damaging one's health.

Our new electronic environment.

These magnetic devices will provide a certain amount of enhanced protection to your system. However, there is much yet to be done in this direction as I will explain in a moment.

We depend on electricity for almost everything. We live in a world which is increasingly run and organised through electricity. This has given rise to a multitude of electrical machines which have become part of the fabric of our daily lives. The use of computers, televisions, central heating pumps, fluorescent lights, photocopiers, washing machines, radios and bedside lamps, plus a host of other equipment, have created a huge web of electrical wiring in every house, factory, public building and office. This complex new environment can have serious effects on our general health and well being.

This is because the method of power generation used in almost every electrical device or system in use on the planet today is creating artificial spiral vortex fields at right angles to the current flow which rotate in the opposite direction to the ones which occur naturally and are used within living systems.

In the human system, rhythmic patterns of activity throughout the organism are of a left-handed nature, they are the result of the movement of force fields which initially organised amino acid/matter into left-handed structures. These left-handed forces, the product of a natural magnetic field, continue to operate in a healthy body. When they are subjected to interference from fields rotating in the opposite direction, a break down in the signals can occur. Aberrant signals emanating from an oscillator in a disturbed pattern can bring about profoundly different growth instructions in single cells and this is nowadays a major stressor which can lead to cancerous states in the body. This is because the cells are receiving the wrong growth instructions from the DNA (which a normal function has a left-hand rotation) which is being stimulated by the wrong signals.

How to protect yourself.

It is vital to good health and particularly to longevity to learn now how to protect yourself against the modern mechanically driven electromagnetic environment.

The planet is a 6 sextillion metric ton battery that is constantly being replenished by solar radiation, lightning and heat from its molten core. The rhythmic pulsations of natural energy flowing through and from the surface of the earth to the protective shields of the Van Allen belt, keep the biological machinery of life on earth running in rhythm and balance.

Each living creature is a collection of dynamic electrical circuits and in the complexity of our bodies, trillions of cells constantly transmit and receive energy in the course of their programmed bio-chemical reactions.

Our hearts, brains, nervous systems, muscles and immune systems are prime examples of electrical systems operating within our bio-electrical body. In a study published in 2005 by electrical engineer Roger Applewhite, two significant factors were confirmed:-

1. Electrons move from the body to the earth and vice-versa when the body is grounded. The effect is sufficient to maintain the body at the same negative-charged potential as the earth.

2. Grounding dramatically reduces the impact of electromagnetic fields on the body.

The Applewhite study showed the protective effect of earthing against environmental electric fields and in his classic lectures on physics in the early 1960s, Nobel Prize physicist, Richard Feynman describes the earth's subtle energies. The surface, as we have seen, has an abundance of electrons which give it a negative charge. If you're standing outside on a clear day wearing shoes or standing on an insulating surface, there is an electrical charge of some 350 volts between the earth and the top of your head if you're about 6 feet tall. That is to say, zero at ground level and 350 volts in the area of your head.

You don't get a shock because air is a relatively poor conductor and has virtually no electrical current flow.

If, on the other hand, you're standing outside in your bare feet, you are earthed, your whole body is in electrical contact with the earth's surface.

Your body is a relatively good conductor. Your skin and the earth's surface make a continuous charged surface at the same electrical potential. Therefore, any object in direct contact with the earth essentially becomes part of the earth and resides within the protective umbrella of the earth's natural electric field.

Accordingly, if you want to protect yourself from the worst effects of the modern mechanically driven electromagnetic environment, then it is important for you to walk barefoot on the earth for at least half an hour each day.

Earthing is dose related.

The longer you are able to ground yourself in your daily life, the more stable, energetic and robust your body functions will be and the greater your ability to heal. The reason for this is that the human immune system evolved over millions of years. During this great span of time, we lived mostly in barefoot contact with the earth. We were naturally earthed. This meant that the biological clock of the body was continually calibrated by the pulse of the earth that governs the circadian rhythms of all life on the planet.

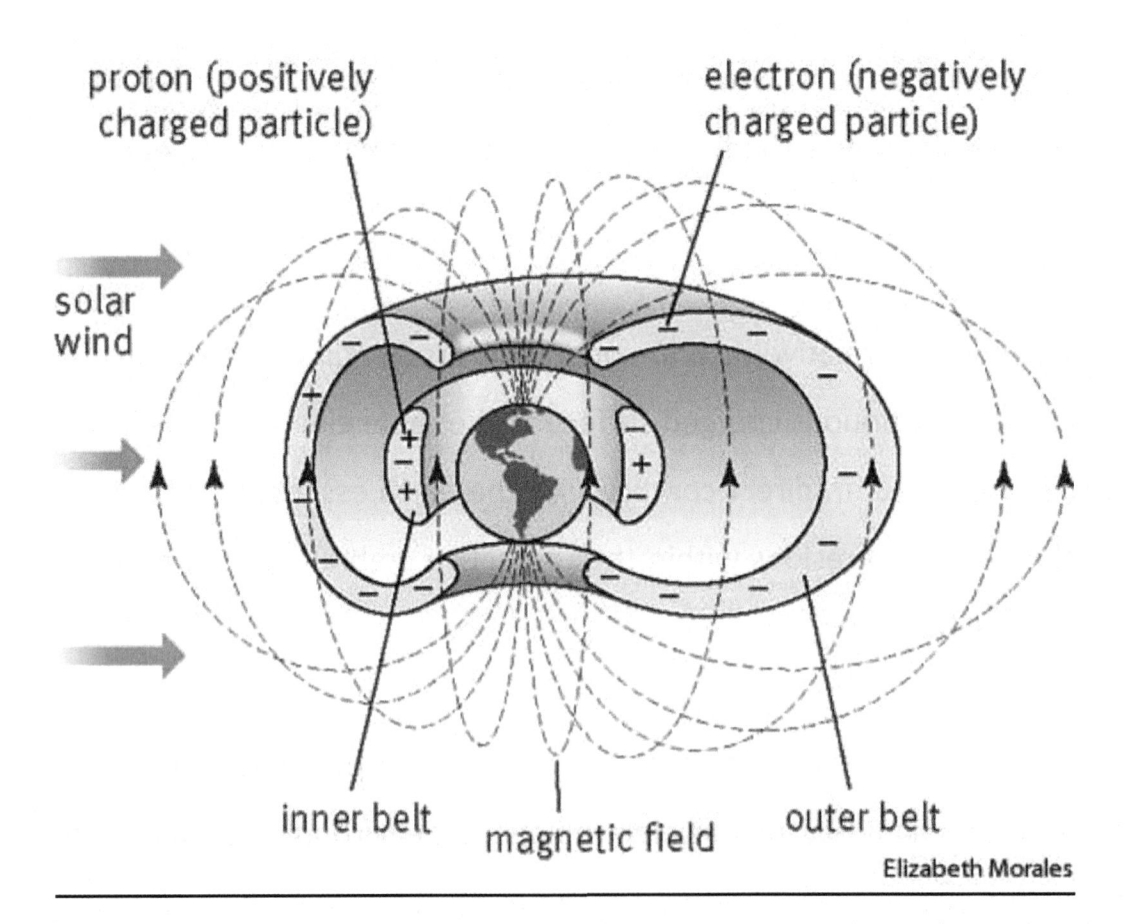

proton (positively charged particle)   electron (negatively charged particle)

solar wind

inner belt   magnetic field   outer belt

Elizabeth Morales

Disconnecting.

What happens to the human body when it's separated from the subtle evolutionary signals from the earth was dramatically shown by experiments in Germany at the world famous Max Planck Institute during the 60s and 70s.

Researchers intentionally isolated volunteers for months at a time in underground rooms electrically shielded from the rhythms in the earth's electrical field. Patterns of body temperature, sleep, urinary excretion and other physiological activities were carefully monitored. All the participants developed a variety of abnormal or chaotic patterns. They experienced disturbed sleep and waking patterns, out of sync hormonal production and overall disruption in basic body regulation.

Whilst we don't live underground, as did these experimentees, we live above the ground and on the ground but we've disconnected ourselves from these bio-rhythms by wearing shoes.

The late Dr. William Rossi, a Massachusetts podiatrist and footwear industry historian, wrote in a 1999 article in Podiatry Management: "A natural gait is biomechanically impossible for any shoe wearing person, it took 4 million years to develop our unique human foot and our consequent distinctive form of gait – a remarkable feat of bio-engineering. Yet in only a thousand years and with one carelessly designed instrument, our shoes, we've warped the pure anatomical form of human gait, obstructing its engineering efficiency, afflicting it with strains and stresses and denying its natural grace of form and ease of movement head to foot".

He further wrote in Footwear News in 1997: "The Sole (or Plantar Surface of the Foot) is richly covered with some 1,300 nerve endings per square inch. That's more than found on any other part of the body of comparable size and is there to keep us in touch with the earth. The real physical world around us".

The paws of all animals are equally rich in nerve endings and the earth is covered with an electromagnetic layer from which every living thing including human beings draws energy.

The energy residing on the surface of the earth is primarily electrical and the central theme of this part of this paper is that we draw electrical energy through our feet in the form of free electrons fluctuating at many frequencies. These frequencies reset our biological clock and provide the body with electrical energy. The electrons themselves flow into the body, equalising and maintaining it at the electrical potential of the earth.

The original light weight soft sole, heelless and simple moccasin – a piece of crudely tanned leather that envelopes the foot and is fastened on with rawhide thongs – is possibly the closest we've ever come to an ideal shoe. It dates back more than 14,000 years.

To substantiate this, Dr. Morris Ghaly measured the circadian secretion of cortisol on people before and after they slept grounded over a period of a few weeks. The study was published in a 2004 issue of the

Journal of Alternative and Complementary Medicine and the conclusion was:-

Earthing during sleep resynchronises cortisol secretion more in alignment with its natural, normal rhythm – highest at 8am and lowest at midnight.

Whether you sleep grounded or walk barefoot on the earth, the effect of earthing out all of the unnatural energies impacting your body's antenna is profoundly beneficial.

Blood Thinning.

Experiments conducted by Stephen Sinatra MD with a group of clinical physicians, PhD's working in the medical field, nurses and the author Clint Oba showed an astonishing effect on blood viscosity of grounding.

This experiment involved taking a drop of blood before and after 40 minutes of grounding by electro patches, and then examining the fresh unstained blood under a dark field microscope.

The after-grounding picture showed that people's blood dramatically changes within a short period of time after an individual is in contact with the earth. Specifically, there were considerably fewer formations of red blood cells associated with clamping and clotting. The blood appeared to be thinner.

The result suggested that individuals with heart disease and inflammatory thick blood (typical in cardiovascular disease and diabetes) may reap huge benefits from simply earthing themselves on a regular basis.

Inflammation and ageing.

Inflammation comes in two forms, acute or chronic. The acute form takes place as an initial response to the body to harmful stimuli. It involves the mobilisation of plasma from the blood into the injured tissue and in the short-term this is a beneficial reaction.

On the other hand, chronic inflammation means a progressive shift in the type of activity going on at the site of the inflammation.

This occurs when you get simultaneous destruction and healing of the tissue, but also a harmful free-radical encroachment into healthy surrounding territory.

(Free radicals are the basis of chronic disease and the ageing process, particularly accelerated ageing and limited lifespan.)

This occurs when normal inflammation veers out of control because of the lost contact with the earth. People are suffering from an electron deficiency, that is to say not enough free electrons on hand to neutralise the rampaging free-radicals. Unfortunately, these go on to attack the adjacent healthy tissue in an ever expanding vicious cycle. The non-stop attack mode generates an auto-immune response manifesting as chronic inflammation and the immune system has run amuck. The pain generated in this process is entirely due to the positive free radical reactions and can be considerably assuaged by continually earthing the system/body on a regular basis.

Earthing then considerably benefits each and every one of us, reduces chronic pain, energises us, reduces or eliminates jet lag, dramatically speeds healing and helps prevent bed sores, lessens hormonal and menstrual problems, accelerates recovery from intense athletic activity, thins blood and improves blood pressure and flow. It normalises the body's biological rhythms, lowers stress and promotes calmness in the body by cooling down the nervous system and stress hormones. It improves sleep and protects the body against potentially health disturbing environmental electromagnetic forces.

To conclude, the wearing of magnetic bracelets and similar devices is highly beneficial as we have seen, as is the practice of earthing on a daily basis. It's now possible to buy special sandals which will earth you automatically and equally possible to buy bed sheets which either plug into earth systems in the house or can be attached to copper rods driven into the ground to earth your body and pick up the earth's natural rhythms whilst sleeping.

Magnetic field.

During the last 500 years the Earth's magnetic-field strength has decreased by about 50% and Dr. Nakagawa of the Isuzu Hospital, Tokyo, Japan has written a thesis entitled: "Magnetic Field Deficiency Syndrome and Magnetic Treatment". In this thesis he points out and lists syndromes of modern people that he relates to magnetic field deficiency. Dr. Nakagawa believes that the current trend of the decreasing strength of the earth's magnetic field is creating magnetic field deficiency syndrome since he believes that there is a direct relationship between the decrease in the earth's magnetic field acting on the human body and the improvement of abnormal conditions of the human body by the application of magnetic fields.

Given that this is now a well-proven hypothesis in practice, it is then well worthwhile wearing a magnetic health device so as to preserve your internal electromagnetic environment and health.

THE HUMAN ANTENNA.

Our blood, as I've said, has the same composition as sea water of the Cambrian period. The same salts that are present in sea water are present in all of us as, is the same sensitivity to the oscillations of our surroundings to a greater or lesser degree. This has had a substantial bearing on our evolution. Evidence from magnetised rocks show that the earth's field strength has varied considerably in the past and this variation has had a considerable influence both on our behaviour and on our evolution.

Here's how.

The magnetic fields of the moon and the sun plus the effects of the solar wind's magnetic field, induce a magnetic field in the earth of a strength depending on its mineral content, their relative distances, and the state of the intervening electrolyte, the air.

Since an electric current is induced in any conductor moving in a magnetic field, the mineral content of the conductor has a bearing on the degree of conductivity.

Humans are such a conductor moving in the earth's magnetic field and the current induced in our blood, by virtue of continuous movement, supplies oxygen to the lungs and tissues and most plentifully to the brain. The brain transmits energy to the nerves and muscles by means of electric impulses and so the strength of the magnetic field affects our response.

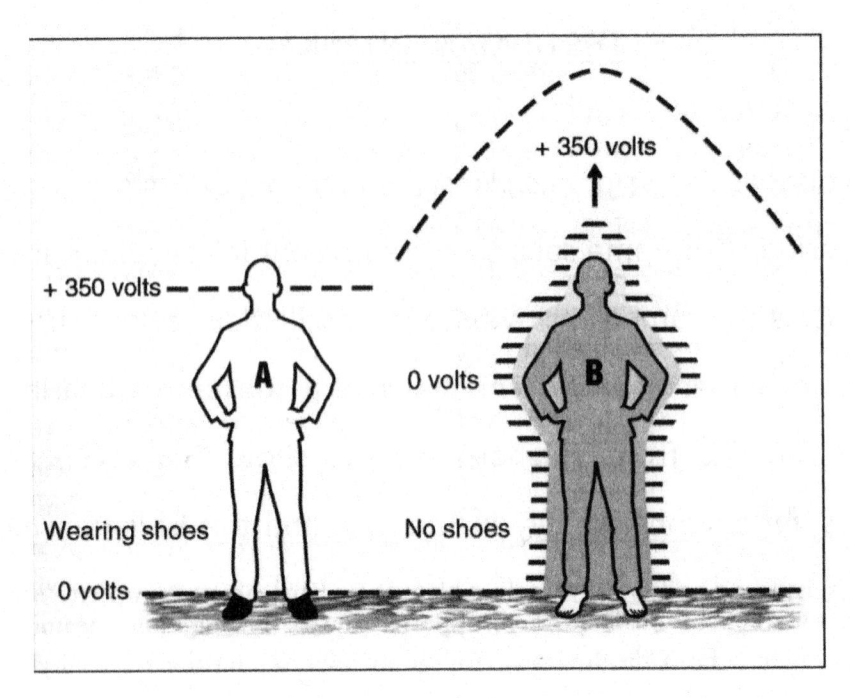

The 'umbrella' effects of earthing (*Earthing*, ISBN 978-1-59120-283-7)

Blood is conditioned by diet, exertion and the behaviour of the other organs in the body and is also liable, as a conductor in the earth's magnetic field, to changes in that field which may sometimes make it exceed or fall below its normal pH.

As we've seen earlier, alterations in the pH, which currently averages between 7.3 and 7.4, will produce corresponding changes in the activity of the brain and nervous system. Departure from the normal alkalinity of the blood, a change in pH, is well shown by nervous disturbances.

Increasing alkalinity leads to an excessive neuromuscular irritability which is known as tetany, preceded by headaches, nausea and mental confusion and also lassitude.

On the other hand, a failure to maintain alkalinity leads to extreme breathlessness, stupor and with terminal coma.

Ancient Civilisations.

The peoples who built the great civilisations of the eras before the first millennium BC were differentiated from us by a physiological factor which influenced the conductivity of their bodies, so that changes which we can only detect by sensitive instruments when we are in normal health, were then perceptible by the brain.

The changes which have taken place in our physiology and behaviour over the millennia are directly linked to changes in the earth's electromagnetic field.

Such changes, no doubt, occurred very gradually by changes in the mineral content of man's blood and account for the cultural and anatomical changes detected by anthropologists in the history of mankind, dividing flint-users from copper, copper from bronze-using man and bronze from iron.

For example, the early Egyptian civilisation was based upon the use of copper, iron only being available from meteorite sources. The Egyptians recording something in the region of 14,000 years of practice in their religion seemed to be dominantly concerned with balancing, explaining and making allowances for man's changing levels of excitability brought about by the general anaemia in our species at that time.

The mineral content of a living creature is the most important component of their resistance to electrical stimuli. Since conductivity is a reciprocal of resistivity, it must be increased where resistivity is low. Resistance of the human body depends principally on the mineral content which is contained largely in the blood and bones. So man's conductivity will be increased when his resistivity is low as it is in anaemia. Copper is a much better conductor than iron and far less retentive so that one might expect the metabolism of an anaemic person to be affected and his behaviour to be more impulsive and changeable, more susceptible to exogenous electrical rhythms such as those of the earth's field or of an artificial magnetic field.

As we've seen, there was very little iron in early Egypt but an abundance of copper. With the introduction of iron which is a constitution of haemoglobin and much more retentive than copper, there came about a profound change in human behaviour. Up to the introduction of iron across the board in human society, human kind was chiefly vegetarian and relatively anaemic. However, when the blood of our species became concentrated by the increase of protein, that is to say, by the consumption of much more meat in our diet, and further stabilised by the addition of iron, then sensitivity decreased, man became more independent of his environment, longevity fell away dramatically and society changed visibly.

Cro-Magnon.

35,000 years BC in south-west Europe more or less in the shadow of the Pyrenees, the first and most enduring of all human civilisations existed and lasted for an astonishing 25,000 years.

This stone-age civilisation created by the first really modern Europeans, was more long-lasting than any that had succeeded it. It was ten times longer than the reign of the Pharaohs in Egypt, 25 times longer than the thousand years of Greco-Roman history and extraordinarily durable.

Although the historical lineage of humankind stretches much further back (5 or 6 million years) it left nothing behind other than stone implements with which they broke open nuts and butchered what they had hunted.

The arrival of mankind in south-western Europe was the culmination of the great migrations, a hundred thousand years earlier, which caused modern Homo sapiens to leave his African homeland and spread outwards to every corner of the earth.

Cro-Magnon was the first to leave behind an image of his civilisation and back in those days we were great technical innovators. Whilst our predecessors' stone tools had scarcely changed in a million years, we invented the spear thrower, the harpoon, lamps to illuminate caves and drills that could put an eye in a needle, along with ropes to bind tents together.

This burst of creativity shows that Cro-Magnon was not simply an improved version of his early ancestors but was a totally unprecedented entity who inaugurated the first and most astonishing of all human civilisations.

Whereas, we have the knowledge and technology of earlier civilisations to draw upon, the genius of the Cro-Magnon is that they worked it all out for themselves. We know that the Sahara desert began to form around a hundred thousand years ago, and that large swaths of the northern African part of the continent began to dry out. This was probably the cause of the great diaspora of humankind from Africa, along the coastal byways to colonise the rest of the world. And we also know that this period of drying out was dependent entirely upon solar activity i.e. the greater intensity of the sun having the effect of drying out large areas of the habitable section of the globe. (By habitable section I mean those areas between the tropics of Cancer and Capricorn which were not then subjected to the ice age).

The rapid changes in our species brought about by the stressful necessity of migration may well be one of the causes of the sudden explosion of creativity in Cro-Magnon but, certainly up until that time and even beyond, humankind was still predominantly anaemic subsisting in the main on an alkaline diet.

With the coming of the various metal ages, mankind certainly became more excitable. This excitability brought about by an extreme sensitivity to fluctuations in the electromagnetic environment, clearly gave rise to various great religious imperatives at the heart of which is a desire to comprehend, regulate and ascribe power to the influences of the environment. At that time solar worship and lunar worship were dominant long before monotheism gained ground.

Iron.

The introduction of iron on a large scale within human civilisation effected a profound turning point in human development since its ubiquity introduced high levels of haemoglobin into the blood of our species, which in turn made us more "down to earth" and much more aggressive.

This aggression stems from an alteration in the alkaline balance of the blood where a higher incidence of haemoglobin will mean that less oxygen is absorbed / available which causes the entire system to acidify.

Another factor which is cohort in this change is the fluctuations in the earth's magnetic field over this time.

The relationship between man's behaviour, his electro-chemical makeup and his environment are well grounded in science as we've seen and the explosion of our aggressive, short-lived species across the planet in recent millennia is largely due to the profound change in our nature which took place at the collapse of the Bronze Age when iron began to dominate our lives.

The simplest way to reduce the influence of iron on your bloodstream is to eat with bronze knives and forks, to plough the land or till the earth with hardened copper implements and to cook in copper or tin pots.

The reason for this is that minute quantities of iron scrape off steel eating utensils, are scoured off iron and steel cooking pots, thus entering our system. Equally, soil structure is reduced, in effect "shorted out", by the use of steel or iron gardening implements, ploughs and the like, the fertility of the soil being considerably enhanced by the use of copper. These are well known bio-dynamic remedies and they work.

Ultimately, what we are concerned with in seeking enhanced longevity is a more efficiently functioning human antenna. This because it is the steady rhythmic fluctuations in the planet's energy which entrain, stimulates and maintains life. Reduce the functioning of the antenna by bad diet etc. and you reduce your lifespan. Increase it and you increase your lifespan!

The human frame is a superb antenna being composed of about a fathom of salty water. This is an excellent electrolyte, in other words it carries and transmits the vast range of frequencies which surround us in this world. This outer electrolyte surrounds the spinal column and the spinal cord is made up of almost pure Vitamin C which, as we've seen from the earlier chapters, is a fantastic conductor.

On top of this accumulator/battery-like structure there sits a cranium in which resides a brain, once again a room temperature superconductor and this very housing, the skull, has a profound role to play in this antenna-like structure as we shall see.

Magnetic lines of force.

The earth has the properties of a large magnet and generate streams of magnetic energy that follow lines of force. If you turn on any motor or generator you can hear its energy at work since it will hum as it revolves. This hum is associated with the energy itself and not so much the movements of the rotor through the air. If the motor stalls while the power is turned on, the hum will become louder! The electrical and magnetic forces in the motor generate the sound waves. The earth itself acts as a giant dynamo and produces similar sound waves revolving as it does one revolution every 24 hours. The hum that the earth, acting as a dynamo, produces is at a very low frequency, a low vibration and thus it goes unnoticed as we go about our daily lives. It is our planet's inaudible fundamental pulse or rhythm.

There are a great many pulses and rhythms at work within this structure of the earth since any change in the density of an elastic medium can serve as a source for sound. The earth's energy includes mechanical, thermal, electrical, magnetic, nuclear, and chemical action, each a source of sound.

The most common sound waves are produced by the mechanical vibrations of solids, liquids and gases. Solid vibrators include strings and rods, membranes and plates, shells, bells and three dimensional extended objects like the earth itself.

Known as the Schumann resonances, there are fundamental vibrations which are the result of electrical activity between the earth and its upper atmospheric layers. Collectively known as electromagnetic cavity, the elements that make it up are the earth, the ionosphere, the troposphere and the magnetosphere. The fundamental frequency of the vibrations is calculated to be 7.83 hertz with overlaying frequencies of 14, 20, 26, 32, 37 and 43 hertz.

Resonance and harmonics.

Most of these sound frequencies are well below our levels of hearing, but nevertheless have a profound effect on our lives, our emotions and our energy levels.

Their energies resonate within us and indeed we are formed of harmonic structures which are the basis of these resonances.

To understand resonance, it's best to use the analogy of a piano.

Press down a key or several keys forming a chord, without actually striking the note, then undamp the strings by pressing the loud pedal. Play the corresponding note on an octave higher and the strings you have opened on the lower octave will vibrate in sympathy. If you hum into the piano in the same pitch, the strings will again respond. This transfer of energy is due to resonance. The transmission of energy and vibration go hand in hand. The strings of a musical instrument are induced to vibrate, and the energy reaches our ears in the form of sound waves.

When airborne sound forces mechanical vibrations in several piano strings that vibrate at different frequencies, the phenomenon known as harmonics is at work. Elements will absorb energy from a source more efficiently if they're of the same frequency. Multiples of the fundamental forcing frequency, known as harmonic frequencies, will also efficiently absorb this energy and vibrate in their natural resonance.

This is why soldiers are instructed to break step when marching across a bridge because each step of an individual soldier acts as a force on the bridge. If the rest of the company joins this soldier in marching together across the bridge, the energy provided by that one step is amplified many times over and the bridge will vibrate in time to the march.

The pounding of feet on the bridge is known as the forcing frequency and if this frequency happens to coincide with the natural frequency at which the bridge resonates, the absorption of energy will be maximised and the vibration of the bridge will become much greater up to the point where it can shake itself apart. This is explained in the Encyclopaedia Britannica:-

If the damping is very small, a vibrator will draw correspondingly large average power from the source, especially resonance. If the damping becomes effectively zero or even negative, as can happen under certain peculiar circumstances, the power withdrawal may become so great as to lead to a runaway vibration that may destroy the vibrator.

A coupled oscillator.

The human body when earthed (i.e. in its bare feet) forms a coupled oscillator that is in harmonic resonance with the earth. A coupled oscillator is an object that is in harmonic resonance with another, usually larger vibrating object. When set into motion, the coupled oscillator will draw energy from the source and vibrate in sympathy as long as the source continues to vibrate.

It's been known for some time that vibrations at around 6 hertz influence the brain and produce various effects in humans and we now know in fact that the brain frequencies entrain with the Schumann resonances across their full spectrum.

NASA consultant and acoustic engineer, Tom Danley, has identified four frequencies which form an F sharp chord which is said to be the harmonic of our planet. And in the same way that a bell is tuned to a fundamental hum and its harmonics removed by removing metal from the critical areas, these low volume frequencies are the forcing frequencies which have shaped mankind's development into the species that we are today. More of which later.

To bring things to a head!

The human skull could be described as being generally round with an aperture on one face, is connected to the spine which we've already seen is a superb transmitter of information received throughout the body. The human skull is fundamentally a Helmholtz resonator which responds to vibrations and actually maximises the transfer of energy from the source of the vibrations. A resonator is normally made out of metal but it can be made out of any other materials and a classic example of a Helmholtz resonator is a hollow sphere with a round opening that is one-tenth to one-fifth the diameter of the sphere.

The size of the sphere determines the frequency at which it will resonate. If the resonant frequency of the resonator is in harmony with the vibrating source, such as a tuning fork, it will draw energy from the fork and resonate and at a greater amplitude than the fork is able to do without its presence. In other words, it forces the fork to greater energy output than what is normal, or "loads" the fork. Unless the energy in the fork is replenished, its energy will be exhausted quicker than it normally would be without the Helmholtz resonator. But as long as the source continues to vibrate, the resonator will continue to draw energy from it. Thus we regard the ever vibrating earth as the resonator and the human structure as the antenna/Helmholtz resonator we can see that energies emanating from the ever vibrating planet are drawn in and utilised by the human form both as a source of energy and structural arbiter.

By way of reinforcing what I'm saying here, I point to the fact that human babies put on an initial spurt of growth after their birth and put on weight well in excess of the amount of food that they take in.

Further yet, astronauts and also people confined in nuclear submarines for great lengths of time, both groups exhibit disorientation, loss of bone growth and general deterioration until returned to the normal surface environment.

In his classic text, "The Geomagnetic Field and Life" by the Russian scientist Alexander Dubrov, Professor Dubrov combines western studies with extensive research in eastern Europe over the last 20-odd years and provides general support for the field and resonance concepts of this work. He regards the moment at which an organism begins to grow, and the specific interaction of genetic and molecular polarities with a geomagnetic field, as of fundamental importance to its future development. The geomagnetic forces are essentially life-giving, while the complementary gravitational forces stabilise these effects.

If we think of genes not as static on-off groups of chemicals, but as oscillators with coherent frequency properties, then there's no inherent theoretical problem about embryonic growth. An ordered set of oscillators will produce a consistent patterning of material. It will ensure that the formation of new structures will occur according to definite time sequence. It will create patterns of rhythmic activity throughout the organism. It can account for degeneration and ageing as well as the initial growth patterns. It can explain in principle both the cell formation and the whole body formation.

There is now considerable experimental evidence that the geomagnetic field modifies genes and chromosomes (there is for instance a gene mutation of the insect Adalia which changes the wing colour from red to black and which changes correlate quite closely with the geomagnetic field. In versions of the x-chromosomes of the fruit fly have been shown to follow gmf fluctuations). We now know that low frequency fields can affect mental states, physiological functions, bone structure, general patterning processes and germ plasma. These fields or vibrations directly affect a larger structure like the cell membrane which has unusual electromagnetic properties and also relate to unusual water structures in the cell membrane, these being sensitive to low frequency fields.

Summary.

Our species development, health and lifespan are modulated and moderated by the geomagnetic field which expresses all the rhythms of vibration which derive from a very active planet. Thus, we are creatures intended by a life force to be in harmony with our planet and in order to be in harmony it is necessary to have as clean and properly functioning an antenna as possible.

It is also essential to keep in close touch with the planet's fundamental forcing frequencies to have mind to this as a constant in our lives which affects the length of our lives.

The phrases we use in everyday language such as being off-key, off-colour, in-tune, keyed-up and so forth present our basic understanding of the forces which bear upon us and which formed us and yet as a species we have diverged far from our healthy bond with our environment, the consequence of which is that we reap the bitter harvest of a foreshortened life.

EXERCISE FOR LONGEVITY.

Since we are nowadays unable to follow the wondering lifestyle of the hunter-gatherer for which we are perfectly designed, it behoves us to look at a variety of other exercises which will deliver similar benefits but preferably in a shorter more manageable time.

The first of these is rebounding.

<u>Rebounding</u>.

Rebounding on a small trampoline basically means bouncing up and down for a short period each day and this harnesses three powerful forces - gravity, acceleration and deceleration.

Although your body does not recognise the difference between gravity and acceleration, it does automatically strengthen itself to cope with the worst conditions that it repeatedly encounters. Consequently, when you're putting your body under an apparent 1½ times normal gravity, it will strengthen itself to a level to cope adequately with this condition. As a result, the body gradually becomes stronger in each cell and, as a consequence of that, all the muscles and organs become stronger. What rebounding does is to harness and use the force of gravity effectively.

At the top of the bounce the body becomes completely weightless and this stimulates the lymphatic flow. This gravity/non-gravity repetition occurs about 100 times each minute, so the body quickly strengthens a little. The lymphatic circulation also improves to bring about greater efficiency in the clearing of waste matter in the body and in the effectiveness of the immune system.

Almost everybody can be fitter by spending a few minutes each day on a rebounder and ten minutes on a rebounder will give you the same benefits as a thirty minute jog (but without the skeletal shock).

NASA – the space agency, says that, "rebound exercise is the most efficient and effective exercise yet devised by man".

You also lose weight, lower you cholesterol, improve your circulation and can rapidly recover from arthritis.

Backswing.

The backswing or incline table is an extremely good form of exercise, particularly as it helps your liver clean up your bloodstream and remove many latent toxins in your body. By attaching your feet to one end of the backswing and raising your arms, you alter the fulcrum or balance point of the device, thus allowing yourself to be inverted. In this head-down position your spine naturally elongates. This is a very beneficial function since, as we age, our spines tend to compress. Thus by drawing them out, we can regain quite a lot of our spinal flexibility and also, by removing the pressure from the synovial fluid in the joints, can help it flow more freely and better lubricate the spine once it's returned to its upright position.

Other benefits which flow from the backswing are substantial. For instance, it reduces back pain and helps the complex of muscles which keep our spines upright to momentarily relax being exercised in the opposite direction to which they normally perform.

Another substantial benefit from using the backswing is the fact that, once inverted, many of the toxins that have built up in your cells and in your lymphatic system are "dumped" back into your bloodstream whence, from which, they are cleaned by your liver and kidneys.

This is a vital long-term function which will make your body more supple, less toxic and considerably more comfortable. Highly recommended for those who sit at a desk for long periods!

<u>Swimming.</u>

We are biologically adapted (as aquatic apes) to swim very well. Swimming exercises almost the entire body and does so in a way which dramatically reduces stresses and strains on the musculature and ligaments. Because swimming uses our inherent skills and also "earths" us, it is the best exercise that we can possibly undertake.

Much of our early development was spent in and out of the sea and the body is perfectly streamlined for this adaptation. Swim a few lengths each day and you are undertaking one of the best cardiovascular exercises there is and you will benefit hugely from it.

If you can, please avoid swimming in chlorinated water. Chlorine is a poisonous gas, your skin is permeable to it and it builds up over time to add yet another toxin to the array which you accumulate during your lengthy life. Try and swim in saline water or in fresh water.

Walking.

Walking upright is a fairly recent biological adaptation for hominids and involves the use of an enormous array of muscles and nerves just to keep us upright. Then to have a couple of kilos of head wobbling around on the top of the spine presents yet more problems to our musculature and these are solved, by and large, by having an incredibly adapted foot. The human foot is unique and is a little-understood structure. However, walking barefoot is its ideal application and since you can combine this with the earthing exercises, I suggest that you walk barefoot for 3 miles each day. If you can't walk barefoot, then walk in simple leather moccasins, since these will both protect the soles of your feet and at the same time allow the rhythms of the earth to stimulate your systems.

Walking brings into play a huge number of benefits, not least of which is the foot pump effect of the valves in your legs which allow the blood to be retained and thus assist it in its upward journey back to your heart. This function is assisted by the flattening effect of the veins underneath your feet which pump the blood back up, through the system of valves in the veins in your legs back to your heart.

Walking is thus THE most beneficial exercise which we can undertake and we age much more slowly if we can undertake this exercise regularly each day.

By improving the circulation in the extremities and also taking pressure off the heart by assisting the circulation, a good walk each day can significantly contribute to a longer life.

Back Ball.

The back ball is something that I invented years ago is a method of ironing out the knots in my spinal column. What you do is take a rugby ball, preferably a rubber one with a rough surface, then sit on the floor, place the rugby ball directly behind you.

Incidentally, it's better to have no clothing on your upper body when you're doing this exercise, since otherwise the clothes get caught up in the ball.

The fundamental of the exercise is that you lay back over the ball and roll your spine up and down on it, thus bringing almost your entire body weight on to the point where the ball is in contact with each particular vertebrae. This has the effect of flexing them in the opposite direction to which they are normally stressed. If you proceed slowly up and down the spine using your weight to exercise yourself, you will find that this exercise is absolutely invigorating.

If at the end of this transit up and down the spine you lay at rest with the spine beneath your pelvis, this then helps to open the pelvis and stretch the stomach muscles to the sides of your body, which in turn helps to strengthen the muscular corset around your lower abdomen.

There are a variety of ways you can finesse this exercise, all of which are available in the book, "Back Ball", copies of which are available on-line.

<u>Sex.</u>

Probably the most enjoyable exercise ever indulged in by our species, sex is a vital marker to good health. If you enjoy a healthy sex life you will be more healthy because there is no better cardiovascular exercise in the world.

As females age, their oestrogen levels decline. This has the effect of making many older women look "mannish" (i.e. like men) simply because as the oestrogen levels fall, they reveal the testosterone levels which have always been present but which have been subsumed by the higher oestrogen levels.

This process can be altered and, in many cases, reversed if the person or persons concerned lead a regular sex life.

In the male, sex is very much of a vital function, since it is important to keep the prostate gland active in producing the liquid which makes up a substantial part of the semen. Where the prostate becomes less active and particularly when it ceases to function, this is usually a precursor condition to significant problems (i.e. prostate cancer).

Our species overall has one major imperative and that is to survive! Any indication that some function is no longer needed, is taken as an indication by the life force that this aspect, or this individual has become redundant and can begin to die.

Ergo, to fool the life force into believing that you are still busy procreating, a healthy sex life, along with all the other recommendations in this series of talks, is a vital necessity as we age.

I am not recommending here that you indulge in chemically induced sex as I think this is a dangerous practice. I am, however, recommending a regular sex life (in whatever form that takes for you) for as long as you are able.

It's worthy of note that there are many tried and tested herbal remedies which can assist you in achieving this ambition and please note herbs are not harsh chemicals, they work on an entirely different level combining as they do a variety of functions with which humankind has attuned over the millennia. In other words, herbal remedies are much better for you because they combine a number of compatible functions which complement each other. The reverse is true of harsh chemical remedies.

If for some reason you are unable to indulge in sex as a prophylactic to old age, the next best thing is teaching. Tribal elders have held down this function for many millions of years and it is the one function you can perform which contributes significantly to the continuum in the spiritual life of our species and which will help keep you young.

SUNLIGHT SLIM AND SUNLIGHT HEALTHY.

In spring the component of ultraviolet light in sunlight increases. As the sun climbs higher in the sky, its rays have to penetrate less of the atmosphere than in winter when it is low on the horizon. This means that the atmospheric shield is reduced in thickness and this allows more UV to reach the surface.

This higher component of UV is the "trigger" that starts growth in plants (and animals) and it also has another important role in life – it stimulates the production of Vitamin D (and C).

Vitamin D comes in two forms – plant vitamin called D2 (ergocalciferol) and animal Vitamin D – D3 (cholecalciferol). Vitamin D is made in animals and humans by sunlight hitting the skin or fur and this sunlight catalyses the conversion of one form of cholesterol (7-dehydrocholesterol) into Vitamin D3. Vitamin D3 is a hormone that provides information to every DNA cell in the human body and is estimated to control over 1,000 genes by turning them on or off.

<u>Without this "information", you begin to close down and ultimately you die!</u>

The reason for this is that all common diseases in humans have as one of their causes (in many cases the main cause) low levels of exposure to sunlight. Low levels of Vitamin D3 are associated with almost every disease known to affect man, which are not caused by genetic mutation.

Obesity is a particular indicator of low levels of Vitamin D3 and here's why:-

At one period in our development we were subjected to fairly harsh winter conditions when plant food was scarce and animal food hard to get. Accordingly, for us to survive until the spring, we went into hibernation when all our systems shut down or slowed down and much of our activity ceased.

We still have this hibernation reflex today but much less strongly than we used to have it.

As the UV component in sunlight diminished in autumn, our bodies manufactured less Vitamin D3. As we manufactured less Vitamin D3, our bodies repair system worked less vigorously and everything about us slowed down, stopping us from expending much energy.

In preparation for hibernation and as our Vitamin D levels reduced, our bodies converted more food into fat as a store of food to see us through the winter. We also exercised far less.

Today when food is abundant we still slow down in winter and don't get enough sunlight. Our bodies therefore don't convert (or ingest) nearly enough Vitamin D3 and a very high proportion of people (80% across the world) are obese and often ill at the same time.

Sunlight on the skin is now demonised as a cause of skin cancer and we're taught to avoid it, yet sunlight in sensible doses can help cure most illnesses because it delivers vital Vitamin D3 to your system.

When I say sensible doses, I'm talking about exposing yourself to the sun before 11am and after 4pm. Between these times the sun is stronger because it's almost overhead and its rays don't have to pass through any great depth of the atmosphere which otherwise acts as a filter, so it can burn you. Sunbathe before 11am and after 4pm and you will lose weight and become much more healthy because your body will manufacture lots of Vitamin D3. This will cause all of your body's repair systems to go into high performance mode.

If you can't sunbathe, then you can safely take Vitamin D3 supplements of up to 20 milligram a day as part of a normal diet and this translates to a person who weighs 50 kilos safely ingesting 50,000 plus international units of Vitamin D3 a day.

Remember, if this seems a lot, whole body sunbathing for just 30 minutes produces 10,000 to 20,000 i.u. of Vitamin D3 in your skin.

Proof of this strategy already exists in the world. Look at the geographical distribution of disease – near the equator where people get plenty of sunlight, there is a lower incidence of diseases such as arthritis, MS, TB, schizophrenia, allergies, heart disease, Parkinson's, etc. etc. (the list goes on and on).

Any common disease in humans is made worse, if not originally caused, by low levels of exposure to sunlight and thus low levels of Vitamin D3 in the blood.

We are creatures of sunlight!

LIVING RESONANCES.

The human body, in common with all other living systems, vibrates or resonates at different frequencies which are centred on different focal points throughout its structure, according to their composition. These vibrations are of a very low order of intensity being created by the movement of electrons within the many circulatory systems of the body. Probably the best known of these circulatory systems is the bloodstream which has a particularly loud vibration that we can hear in our heart beat. Each beat of the heart shapes the whole body, and the body has a characteristic response to this beat which is quite easily measured. The ejection of blood from the heart's left ventricle causes a peak on a graph, while the portion between the large peaks looks irregular. This occurs because the entire body vibrates due to the action of the blood in the aorta, which is the largest artery in the body.

The bloodstream, the lymphatic system, the bile system, the nervous system, the lungs, stomach and trachea, plus hundreds of other systems, all have their own characteristic level of resonance and sound. All of these are very slow and very low frequency sounds. Most of them well below the range of human hearing (otherwise we'd be deafened by our own internal noises).

In the study of yoga for rejuvenation, the rhythm of breathing, 8 times 4 times 8 times 4 is in harmony with the cellular vibration of the blood, muscles and skeletal structure and there are a whole variety of other rhythms and harmonies which flow together in the human structure to form seven major areas of resonance which have, historically, been known as the chakras.

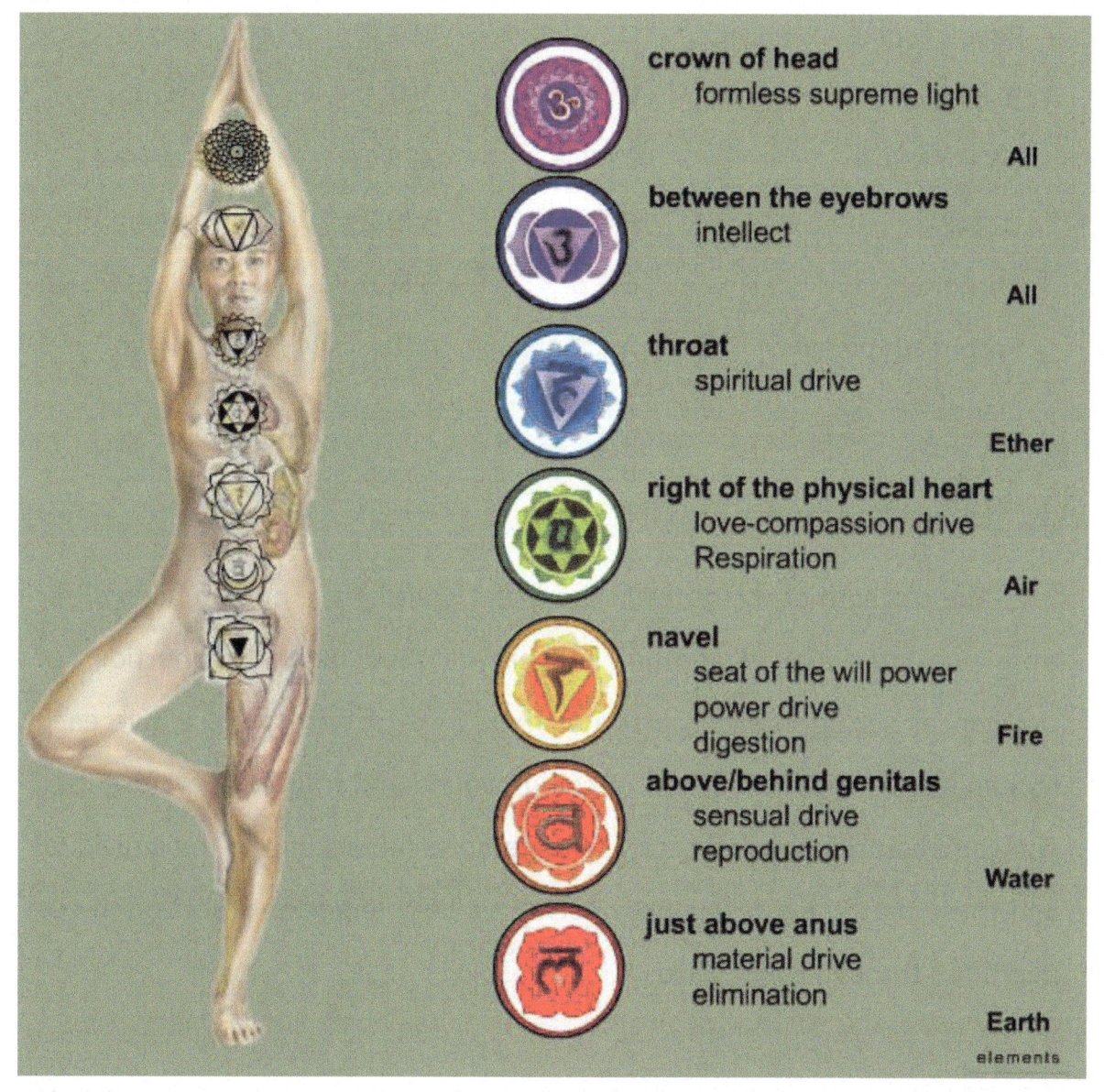

The Chakras

crown of head	formless supreme light	All
between the eyebrows	intellect	All
throat	spiritual drive	Ether
right of the physical heart	love-compassion drive, Respiration	Air
navel	seat of the will power, power drive, digestion	Fire
above/behind genitals	sensual drive, reproduction	Water
just above anus	material drive, elimination	Earth

elements

Each major tone represents the frequencies of all of the resonances within that particular area of the body and is concentrated in a particular focal point or energy centre. Each chakra resonates with a pattern of frequencies that would, if transferred up the electromagnetic scale, produce a series of key-note sounds or colours as follows:-

Energy Centre	Key Note	Cycles Per Second	Colour
Base of spine	C	261.2	red
Spleen centre	D	292.1	orange
Solar plexus	E	329.1	yellow
Heart	F	349.2	green
Throat	G	392.0	blue
Forehead (pineal gland)	A	440	indigo
Crown	B	493.0	violet

The strength of the notes in the major scale of the human body differ from one individual to another and are dictated by the proportions of resonances set up in each person at their time of birth. These give each human being a distinct pattern of colour, sound and fragrance preferences. They also contribute significantly to the emotional makeup of the individual and these patterning resonances perform a very important function in our migration through various lives.

This human cord set up as a resonance structure which owes its structure to the influence of planetary resonances on the human body represents one part of the joined-up relationship between human beings and planet earth.

The earth constantly generates a broad spectrum of vibration and as we've seen that energy is dominant among the formative structures of the human body. When a human being is earthed, as referred to in a previous chapter, all of that energy flows through the body and is an integral component, not only of the immune system but also of the energy systems within the human body.

Physical effects of vibration.

Take, for example, music or sound, this can affect physical processes in the body insofar as it can speed up bodily metabolism, produce exaggerated knee-jerks (in reaction tests), have a marked effect on blood pressure and also the peripheral, and central circulations. It's also been shown experimentally that blood flow to the brain was increased under the influence of music and in the cardiovascular system, pulse rate has been found to increase when the subject was listening to music. Syncopated rhythms are capable of producing a higher pulse rate and there's also evidence that some musical sound such as drumming can drive the pulse rate.

Motor activity.

By monitoring an increase in the number and amplitude of muscle action potentials, it can be shown that muscular activity increases when a subject is listening to music. Similarly, muscle strength can be shown to increase in a strong magnetic field and all of this underlines the fact that we are perfectly capable of drawing energy from our environment provided our bodies are sufficiently receptive to do so.

The resonator.

As we've seen, a coupled oscillator is an object that is in harmonic resonance with another, usually larger, vibrating object. When set into motion, the coupled oscillator will draw energy from the source and vibrate in sympathy as long as the source continues to vibrate. Our bodies act as coupled oscillators drawing energy from the earth and our ability to do this is mediated by the efficiency of our bodily antenna and by the positioning of our bodies in relation to the earth when earthing.

In relation to the earth's magnetic field, human beings are a bit like iron filings scattered upon a plate to which is then applied a magnetic field. We will automatically line up with the lines of force of the magnetic field and all creatures demonstrate this behaviour.

Google Earth has shown that the predominant direction of grazing animals is aligned north to south and when we humans sleep with our bodies aligned north-south (and earthed) we become coupled oscillators able to draw energy from the earth.

In the last several chapters we've dealt exclusively with our evolution and how to clean up your act so as to benefit fully from the application of harmonic power in your life.   Basically, without a clean antenna, you can't function properly, nor draw power from your environment which capability is your birth right.

In the next part I demonstrate precisely how you go about 're-charging your batteries' and I explain in detail the correct way to do this, safely and regularly, so that you can recover your birthright and develop your Harmonic Power.

Welcome to a better future!

HARMONIC POWER

PART IV

HOW TO DRAW ENERGY FROM THE EARTH

©Keith Foster, April 2013

HOW TO DRAW ENERGY FROM THE EARTH

The earth, having the properties of a large magnet, generates streams of magnetic energy that follow lines of force. These electromagnetic forces generated by the earth's rotation radiate outwards from the molten core and exit the surface of the earth to form a shield around the planet known as the magnetosphere. The magnetosphere deflects the solar wind which is the torrent of charge particles thrown out by the sun. If this shield didn't exist we would fry!

Energy broadcast up through the earth's crust, passes through a network of underground streams, lakes, rivers, huge artesian basins and water veins (also through metallic ores).

These water features conduct the energy along specific pathways that they follow. They focus the essentially magnetic energy and collimate it so that it forms specific lines or streams of more intense energy as it leaves the surface.

These energy lines criss-cross the surface of the planet, in some cases remaining in one position for thousands of years depending on the renewal and permanence of the water vein they pass through.

198

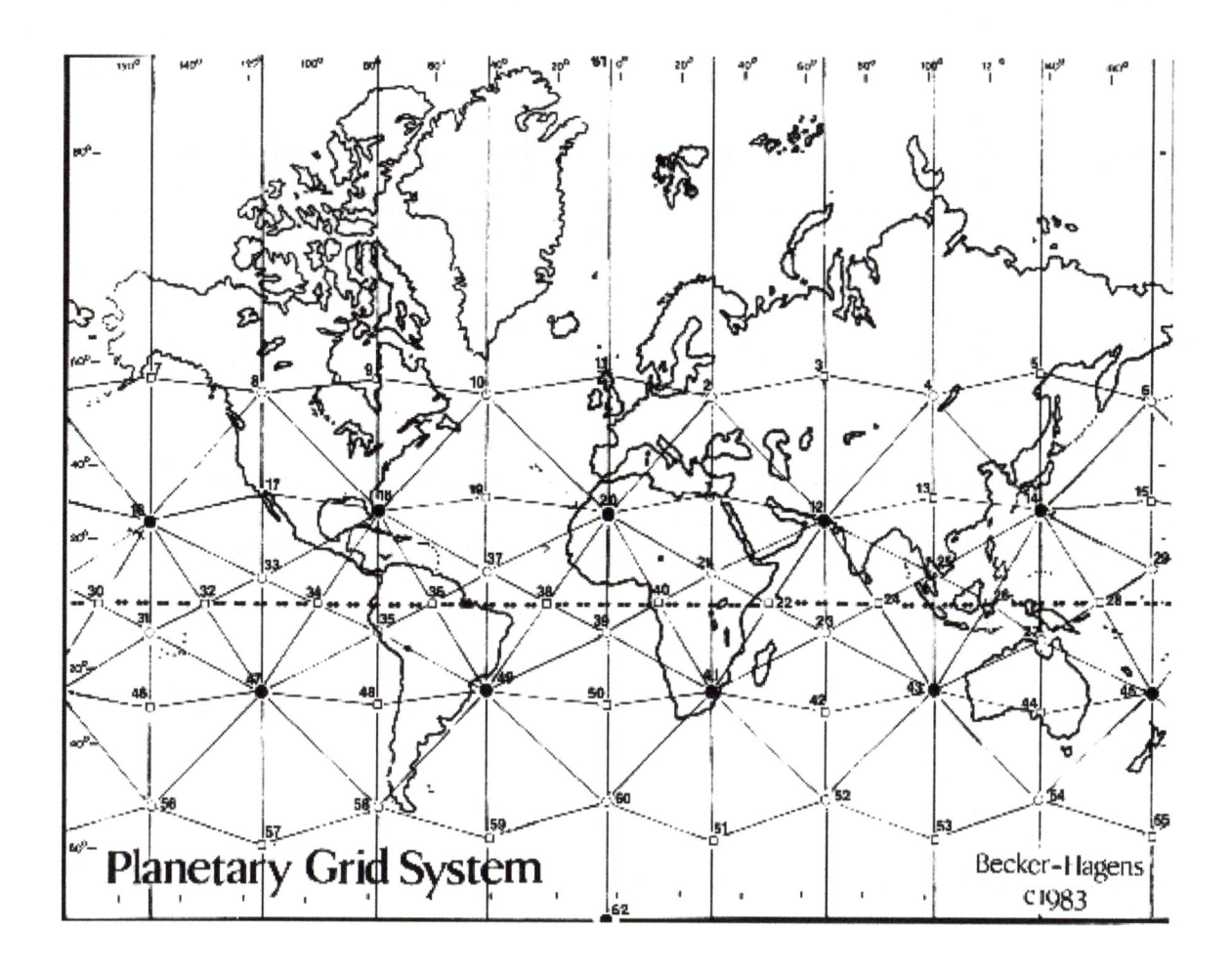

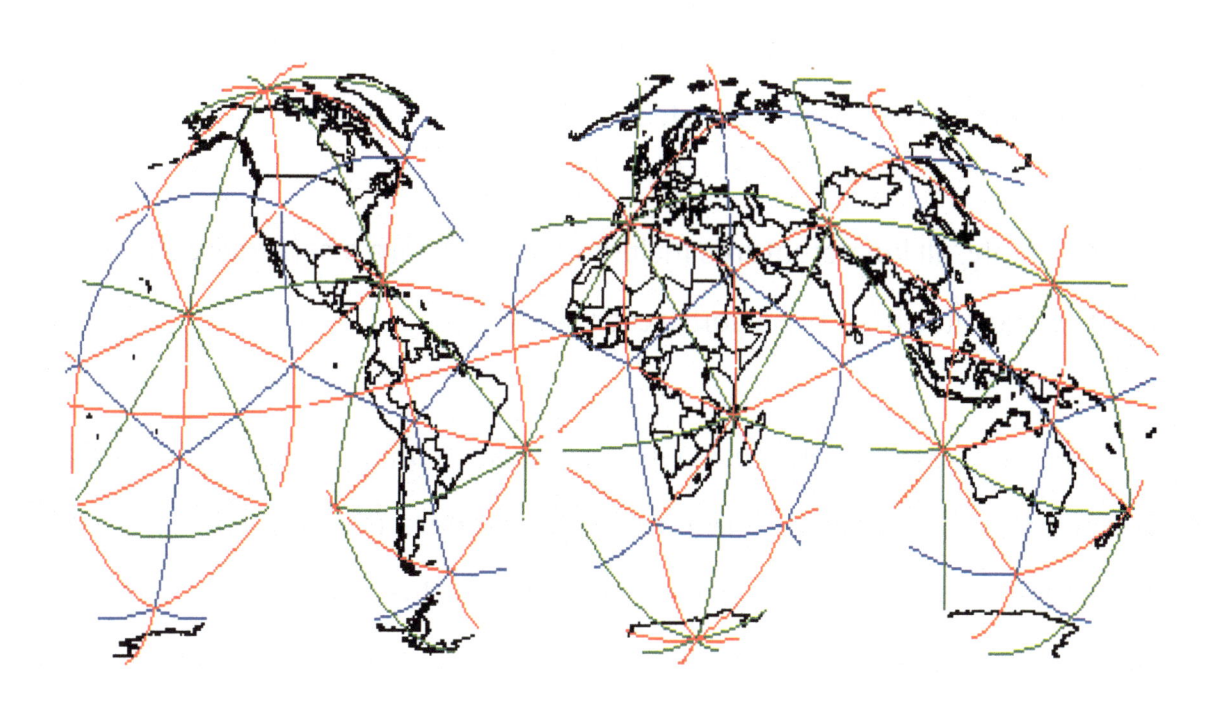

Planetary Grid System

Becker-Hagens
c1983

Earth radiation is part of the natural environment and influences all living things. In 1879 the American physicist E. Hall showed that when blood passes through a magnetic field this sets up minute electrical voltages which carry throughout the body improving cell metabolism and regeneration.

In the case of trees growing on energy lines, it alters the structure of the wood and recent research into avian navigation has shown that, by means of retinal proteins called cryptochromes, birds can actually see magnetic fields.

They perceive these as darker or lighter forms superimposed on the landscape and these help them to navigate in their annual migrations, as well as providing them with an extra energy source.

It has long been known that whales, sharks, eels, salmon and other migratory species navigate using an electromagnetic sensitivity and it's quite probable that they share with the birds and butterflies a built in sensitivity to the geomagnetic profile of their environment.

Certainly, all land creatures including plants share a sensitivity to earth energies and alter their behaviour accordingly.

Since every living structure, when earthed, is an antenna conducting a flow of energy from earth to the upper atmosphere (the ionosphere) then this natural flow of energy is an integral part of all living systems. There are two main contra flows of energy that pass through living systems and these are "pumped" by the moon's diurnal passage over the earth.

When the moon is closest to the earth it compresses the ionosphere towards the surface of the earth and this facilitates the flow of positive charge towards the ionosphere, which has a negative charge on its underside.

Conversely, when the moon wanes the net negative charge at the earth's surface pushes the ionosphere away again (since like charges repel) and that weakens the flow of energy between the earth and the ionosphere.

This energy flow can be seen in action in the diurnal flow of "chi" or "prana" (i.e. electrons) through the acupuncture points in human and animal bodies. It also accounts for the changes in germination and growth rates of plants up to the full moon and down again as the moon wanes.

As energy flows up through the earth's crust it passes through a range of minerals and elements, each of which impart to it a different signature which is why sensitives have been able to dowse mineral deposits etc. from the beginning of time.

However, the earth radiation which concerns us in seeking after power and longevity is that which is given off by energy passing through water lines, water veins.

Fundamentally, there are two distinct types of water which occur naturally on earth, the first of these is the product of the hydrological cycle whereby surface water evaporated from the surface of the sea and falling as rain on land, accumulates in permeable rock basins beneath the surface.

It can then form lakes on the surface also feeding into springs, streams and rivers.

This kind of water has plenty of oxygen dissolved in it and it has a particular characteristic radiation which affects living structures growing or living above it.

The second kind of water is the original water created deep within the rocky mantle of the earth by the combination of gases under great pressure. This water flows in a network of very energetic underground streams and rivers (reminiscent of the flow of blood in mammal bodies or sap in plants). This is the original water of the earth and usually issues to the surface in high altitude springs, particularly in hard rock aquifers or in deep rivers.

This "lymph of the earth" is very energetic and is very oxygen hungry. By absorbing lots of oxygen from the air, it usually doubles in volume by the time it has run out a few metres from its source.

All of the different types of radiation have an effect on living systems and the one which has the predominant effect is that which takes on the signature of live water when it passes through living water veins.

One of the reasons for this is that as this energy radiates from the earth it takes on an anti-clockwise spin. It forms a vortex of energy like a whirlpool in the ether, which affects all living systems that come into contact with it.

At the dawn of time on this planet, the energy driving mechanism for all life developed as the adenosine triphosphate system. This system pumps phosphorus into the mitochondria of each living cell in a process which relies on the anti-clockwise rotation of a bent axle. This acts to pump phosphorus out of the receptacle in which it has bonded with adenosine diphosphate to form adenosine triphosphate. This system is called "boyers binding mechanism".

Every last living cell on the planet uses "boyers binding mechanism" to generate energy and every last cell on the planet is susceptible to energy fields. When these are conducted through their living antenna (bodies) they either drive their systems to produce more energy or place a drag on their system which causes them ultimately to collapse.

So it is that a living system placed on an energy line will be subjected to an unseen but very real electromagnetic force which is rotating in harmony with a dominant energy delivery mechanism in that living system.

This extra spin passing up through the body's antenna, entrains "boyers binding mechanism" causing it to rotate more rapidly, thus delivering much more energy to the living system.

This is the effect we are seeking which, used wisely, can help you to draw significant energy from the earth's vital systems. I say used wisely because whilst you can safely visit this "well" regularly, even daily, it can be overused and overuse can cause damage on a cellular level which can lead to systemic exhaustion and collapse.

I recommend a maximum exposure of 1 hour a day as an energy "top up" and since these energy lines engender higher mental states, I suggest that you use this hour each day for meditation.

To get the full benefit from your regular "top up", you should be "earthed". This facilitates the flow of electrons through your body, which helps clear up any illness you may have. It also enables your body to retain the enhanced energy level for longer after you leave off.

As you go deeper into the practice of The Wisdom Way you will experience greater clarity of thought, a stronger feeling of your own identity and a deeper appreciation of life. You will also (in all probability) avoid disease, be much more healthy and feel calmer, more focused.

However, before going any further, it is very important that you take on board and implement the following information/advice:-

It has been demonstrated by Professor Masasuke Yoshida in Tokyo in 1997, that when the C-sub unit motor which drives the bent axle in the (ATP) adenosine triphosphate system, is induced to run backwards (i.e. clockwise) it burns up the available ATP and the tissue dies.

This very clearly means that if you position yourself over the wrong energy line i.e. one with a clockwise vortex above it, you will harm yourself.

Further yet, if you stay too long on an energy line with the correct rotation of energy, i.e. anti-clockwise, then this will drive your system too hard and exhaust it.

Once your system is damaged in either of these two ways, your vital energy flags and you can become ill! If you sleep over an energy line for long periods, some excellent German research shows that your system can become so run down that you finally succumb to cancer.

Long-term exposure then to any radiant energy can be very dangerous and should be avoided. (A difficult call in our electrified modern world)!

Some species such as cats, ants, oak trees and alder can occupy energy lines with impunity and in fact they thrive on them, even, in the case of cats to preferring to sleep on them. However, almost all other species do not do well on overdoses of energy, so be warned!

How your sensitivity to energy lines works.

Every living thing on earth is sensitive to and can detect electromagnetic fields and energy lines. This sensitivity enables all humans unfailingly to sense a magnetic field produced by a current in the ground of only one microampere
(one over 1,000 of one milliampere) equivalent to a magnetic field change of 10^{12} gauss which is roughly comparable to that of cats which can see in the dark or dogs which can hear ultrasonic frequencies inaudible to any human.

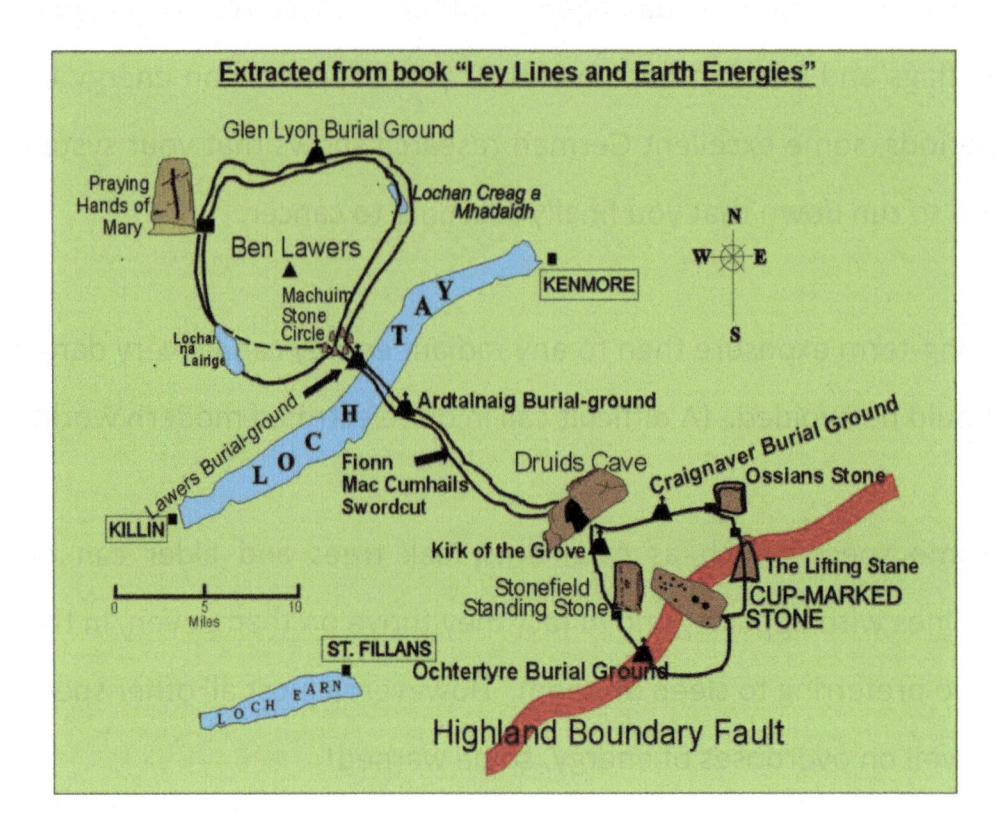

This is a map of two roughly circular leys from a cup-marked stone placed directly over Scotland's Highland Boundary Fault, shown in red.
The HBF is the power source of this ley.

All creation uses these emanations to boost their energy levels when needed and only humankind ignores this ability. However, this was not always so.

Many Roman roads and most, if not all, ancient pathways and holloways follow energy lines. The people who used them and discovered them were clearly sensitive to their properties.

The Romans and the ancient Germanic tribes, along with the Aboriginal people on every continent, use this knowledge extensively and instinctively both to follow energy-rich routes when travelling and to plan the layout of their settlements. No-one camped or slept on these energy lines or roads but they all use them, particularly for long journeys when extra energy came in handy.

In humankind the sensitivity to electromagnetic fields and energy lines is located on two planes which gives it a three dimensional focus. This discovery was pioneered by a Czech-born American physicist, Dr. Harvalik, who used it in his advice to the US army advance material concepts agency when they were teaching divining to the US Marine Corps as a method for detecting roadside bombs during the war in Vietnam.

Dr. Harvalik was able to demonstrate that one electromagnetic sensor was located in the pineal gland and the other in the adrenal glands over the kidneys. Later research into the presence in the pineal and adrenals of magnetically sensitive ferrous molecules has confirmed these findings and this underpins the fact that every human being has the ability to sense energy lines.

Everyone can seek them out and use their power!

The greatest drawback to you using your latent seeking/divining capability is your intelligence. Seeking is an instinctive ability which provides you with access to your sixth sense and any attempt to intellectualise the process is doomed to failure.

Nor is there any right time to "seek" nor a right way to "seek", or a right tool with which to "seek". Rather, you can use anything you can feel comfortable with, any object capable of movement which will respond to changes in your body's response to electromagnetic stimuli.

Pendulums, plumb bobs, L rods made from coat hangers held in the shells of old biro pens from which the ink cartridge has been removed, hazel or willow forks cut from a hedge, a loop of wire held at the ends in both hands with a twist in it, favourite ring suspended on a piece of cotton – almost anything will suffice.

The Practicalities.

Then place your thoughts elsewhere, earth yourself and slowly walk over an area of land and see what happens. At first probably nothing much will occur but persevere – think of it as a kind of walking meditation and relax into it.

When your rods cross or both point in a specific direction, or when your plumb bob or pendulum begins to rotate or your rods to vibrate and point downwards, then you are in touch with an energy line. Walk around that point and mark the direction of the energy line and use your rods or pendulum to establish its direction of flow.

If you feel ridiculous doing this you may care to reflect that once you have rediscovered your innate ability to seek, you will be better able to preserve your life and the lives of your loved ones by moving their beds away from any energy lines that may exist in their bedrooms!

Once you've begun to feel comfortable with your chosen tool, there are two easy short cuts to relearning how to seek.

The first of these is to observe and copy nature.

Find a field where cattle or horses live and see if there is a well defined track which the animals usually follow. It will be quite narrow and well worn. Cross this track at right angles and you will almost always get a reaction from your tool/instrument. This is because animals almost always follow beneficial water energy lines when they have a choice. They are natural seekers.

Then find an area where the cows usually sit. Dowse this and you'll get no reading because animals are always rather good practical seekers and will never rest on an energy line if they have a choice.

The next step is to find an ants' nest. Ants invariably nest on the higher energy points where two lines intercept one another. Walk round this whilst seeking. Walk in ever widening circles preferably marking the point where you get a response, and you will discover the two (or more) energy lines which attracted the ants to that nexus.

In your house you will usually find an energy line crossing point where your cat likes to sleep, but none where your dog feels most comfortable.

Walking the countryside you will always find water energy lines where alder grow and likewise oaks. Particularly oaks, which often line the ancient trods or holloways worn down by the footsteps of generations of our forebears who always followed energy lines.

Be a bit careful here because whilst you are safe in the holloway, you don't want to be caught standing under an oak tree or an alder when there is an electric storm in prospect. Lightening always strikes on water lines and most often on oak trees.

So attracted is the oak to live water energy lines that you will often find ancient oaks covered with cankers at the juxtaposition of two or more energy lines.

The ancients held these ancient oaks to be sacred and they were the focus of many early earth religious practices. This probably reflects in the alleged ability of mistletoe to cure some cancers as it parasites mainly on oak and forms a very high energy radiant cluster.

Incidentally, the multiple cankers on these ancient oaks are a sure sign of an overflow of earth energy being dissipated into the atmosphere by the oak acting as an antenna.

A great many of these ancient oaks growing on high energy lines will have been struck many times by lightening – a sure sign of the existence of an underground flow of living water. These are very good places to meditate and energise yourself provided always that you don't overdo it. Leaning back on an oak tree or clasping an oak tree makes you part and parcel of the huge energy flow of transpiration, particularly on a rising moon.

In your garden a gap in a hedge where nothing will grow is often the sight of an energy line crossing the line of the hedge. Most living systems, especially privet and similar bushes cannot tolerate the high energy levels of water lines. So, close to these gaps is a good place to sit on a chair with your bare feet touching the ground in order to draw energy from the earth. (This helps wonderfully with arthritis).

Other indications are wasps. If you find a wasp nest it's quite probably at the crossing point of two or more energy lines. Similarly, a hive of bees that gives more honey than those around it is almost certain to be on an energy line.

Hens won't perch over energy lines and pigs, often cited as having organs very similar to humankind, are marvellous indicators of the presence or absence of energy lines. Watch them and see if there's a place that they avoid and will not lay down in. Here you will find an energy line or the crossing point of two or more energy lines.

The bottom line here is that all animals, including humankind, are very sensitive to water vein radiation and all can use it to regain energy, to charge up your system.

The other way to seek out an energy line is to use a transistor radio. You can tune it in the mid-500 kilocycle frequency, or wherever else you like, and walk over the ground until you pass over an area where you get a higher level of interference. Walk back and forward around this point until you get the same level of interference from a number of points and you will be standing on an energy line.

You then use your rods or pendulum to seek out and define the direction of rotation of the energy emanating from the line, and once you've found a line where the energy revolves in an anti-clockwise vortex, then you are in business.

Once you've become proficient as a seeker and always assuming that you don't want to sit under an oak tree or that you don't live anywhere where there are plenty of oak trees, then you have to devise a method by which you can ascertain the rotation of the vortices emanating from various earth energies.

There are two ways of achieving this and the best way is to interrogate the energy line using a pendulum or plumb bob.

The low frequency energy coursing through your system when you're standing on an energy line will give either a right-handed or a left-handed spin to your pendulum and you should repeat this at several points down the energy line. If you find it has a right-hand spin (in other words clockwise) move away. If, on the other hand, it has a left-hand spin, then that is a live water energy line where you can afford to then locate your favourite sitting or standing position to re-energise yourself.

Much controversy exists among various dowsing societies as to the various component energies that make up these energy lines (often called ley lines) and, in many cases, they quite rightly warn that one must avoid what they call black lines which can induce cellular deterioration if you linger on them for long periods.

At base, however, the understanding is quite simple to achieve. If you look at the energy flow through and around a bar magnet, you will observe that energy entering the South Pole rotates in a clockwise direction pulling energy into the magnet. However, if you look at the energy emanating from the north pole of the magnet, you will observe that this energy rotates in an anti-clockwise direction pushing energy out of the magnet.

Basically, then when you are standing on an energy line, it wants to be one where the predominant flow of energy is from the earth to the ionosphere in the form of negatively charged electrons rather than the converse which deals with positively charged particles.

The ancients, having a profound knowledge of earth energy and using it in their medicinal practices, were only too aware of the fact that all illness, and all inflammation, respond well and can be alleviated by a flow of electrons, an enrichment of electrons within the cellular structure of the sick person. Since ageing is largely caused by the accumulation of toxins in the body and by the accumulation of the effects of life's excesses, then a health-giving flow of electrons is pivotal to achieving a longer life and this is why the elite in ancient civilisations always made a point of sleeping and indeed living in areas where a concentrated flow of electrons was available to them.

Bronze Age petroglyphs - cup-marked rocks at Ormaig, Kilmartin, West of Scotland

(ref. *Ley Lines and Earth Energies by* David Cowan and Chris Arnold FADO)

Conclusion.

In laying out this wisdom, I should make it clear that the energies I'm talking about are very low frequency energies well below the thresholds that we use in the electronic chaos of our present technology. But then I'm talking of a time when wisdom and well-being were the goals of human society rather than the divisive godless materialism which separates us from our true natures today.

May you enjoy good health!

HARMONIC POWER

PART V

THE GOLDEN AGE

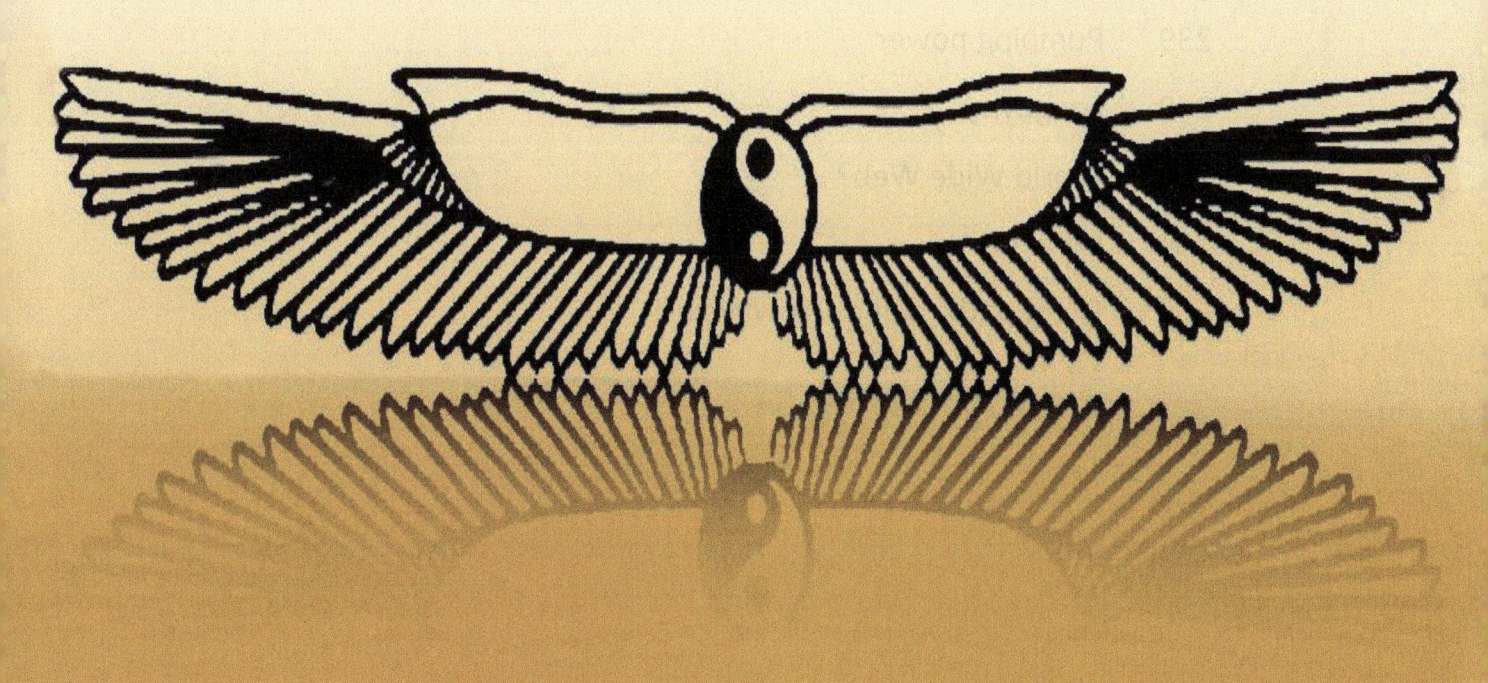

©Keith Foster, April 2013

THE GOLDEN AGE

CONTENTS

Page Number

216	Evidence of an Ancient Civilisation on Earth
228	Why our ancestors built megalithic structures
231	Ley lines
233	Effects on human behaviour
239	Pumping power
248	Longevity
250	World Wide Web?
251	Coral Castle
259	Flight paths and microwaves

EVIDENCE OF AN ANCIENT CIVILISATION ON EARTH.

In 1852 the Reverent Charles Foster (no relative) in his book, *"The One Primeval Language"* ably demonstrates that all the ancient languages (including Chinese) stemmed from one primeval source – Sumer.

More recently it's been shown that very first Egyptian inscriptions employed a language that was indicative of a prior written development, and the only place that had a written language prior to Egypt was Sumer. So Sumer was the cradle of the first civilisation on earth and it is in Sumer that we find the first pyramids known as Ziggurats.

In the broad, flat delta between the Tigress and the Euphrates, there is no stone which could be used to construct these large pyramidal Ziggurats, so they were constructed entirely on bricks made from clay. Far from being small primitive affairs, these Ziggurats were vast, built of mud bricks but covered with a skin of baked bricks set in bitumen. The stage tower of Ur, for instance, measured at its base 60.50 by 43 metres and its sides were slightly bowed, both horizontally and vertically, in order to give the illusion of being straight. This device was long thought to have been invented by the Greek architects who built the Parthenon several thousand years later. But further examination shows it to have originated in Sumer and to have been widely used throughout all the cultures who built the pyramids and observatories, even to the extent of having been used in the construction of the computer/observatory of Stonehenge. Here the huge stone megaliths are tapered in this way, so that they appear as though they have parallel sides.

This method of building slightly convex sides to a building gives an optical illusion of absolute straightness, which is necessary, since if you build it with absolutely straight lines, then this gives the visual appearance of a slightly concave surface, which makes the structure look pinched in the middle.

The Ziggurats were all built to a carefully defined mathematical formula which dictated that they rose through successive stages, each smaller in area and height than the one before but all ending with the highest stage on top. The proportions through the seven stages therefore went as follows:-

Stage One, five and one half; stage two, three; stage three, one; stage four, one; stage five, one; stage six, one; stage seven, two and one half.

Not all Ziggurats were seven stage affairs but the major seven across ancient Sumer were seven stage with various smaller step pyramids being built to serve less complex functions.

If you draw a line through the points or corners on the side of each seven stage Ziggurat, you enclose within that triangle the exact proportions of the great pyramid of Cheops on the Nile. These same proportions occur in all the pyramids or step towers, discovered in all the centres of ancient civilisation. Particularly notable are those in the valley of the Indus, the Mayan Peninsula, Peru and of course ancient Egypt.

The central band around the earth between the tropics of Capricorn and Cancer is littered with highly complex stone structures dating back thousands of years, and the best known of these provide collateral evidence of civilisation existing in great antiquity. It's worth the mention at this juncture that pyramids have subsequently been discovered scattered all around the world and there's a very sound reason for their construction as we shall see.

However, to deal with proof first:-

The pyramidal structures or Ziggurats in Sumer were the first on earth, and the best and most accurate description of the great step pyramid/Ziggurat in Babylon was supplied by Herodotus who was born in around 484BC at Halicarnassus in Asia minor. His great narrative covers the Greco Persian wars, and he travels through the then known world, covering the entire Persian empire, Egypt down to Aswan, Libya, Syria, Babylonia, Susa in Elam, Lydia and Phrygia. He journeyed up the Hellespont to Byzantium, went to Thrace and Macedonia and travelled northwards beyond the Danube to Scythia, eastward along the northern shores of the Black Sea as far as the Don river and some way inland.

He lived in Athens for a time where he met Sophocles and then left for Thorii, the Greek colony in southern Italy sponsored by Athens.

Herodotus' work is an artistic masterpiece and the first complete work of its kind presented as an organic whole. It remains to this day the leading source of original information, not only on Greek history, but on the all important period between 550 and 479BC on the history of western Asia and Egypt at that time.

Herodotus visited Babylon and described the seven stage Ziggurat in great detail, relating how 200 tons of gold were used to decorate the violet and blue glazed room in the seventh stage of the summit. He also describes the colours of the Ziggurat, each stage having a unique colouring, the first being red, the second orange, the third yellow, the fourth green, the fifth blue, the sixth indigo and the seventh violet. In other words, it was constructed proportionate to the resonances within the human body which focus around the different chakras. And it is at this summit just beneath the apex of the pyramid which is the focal point of a variety of highly beneficial energies as we shall see.

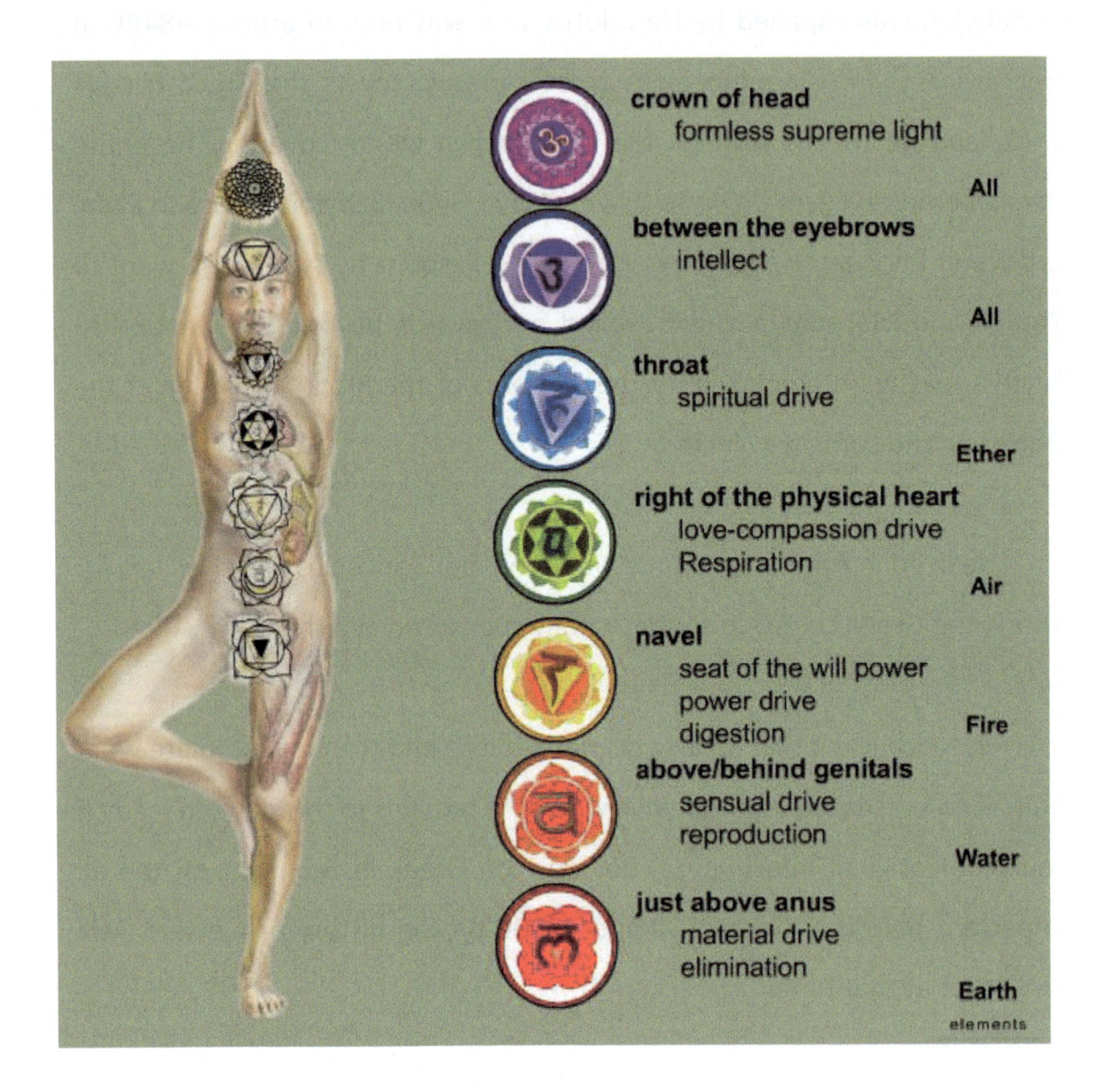

	crown of head formless supreme light	All
	between the eyebrows intellect	All
	throat spiritual drive	Ether
	right of the physical heart love-compassion drive Respiration	Air
	navel seat of the will power power drive digestion	Fire
	above/behind genitals sensual drive reproduction	Water
	just above anus material drive elimination	Earth
		elements

To revert to the collateral evidence of a civilisation existing in great antiquity, we must now refer to book two of Herodotus' history which refers to the priests Thebes showing him 341 huge statues each of which stood for a high priestly generation.

This covers a period of 11,340 years and we know from a variety of evidence that every high priest had his statue made during his own lifetime. Herodotus also tells us that during his stay in Thebes, one priest after another showed him his statue as proof that the son had always followed the father. Egyptian priests assured Herodotus that their statements were very accurate and that they had written records for many generations which covered the 341 statues representing a generation each. This dates the Egyptian civilisation back to the last ice age and there is yet further proof as follows:-

Egyptologists have traditionally believed that the Sphinx and its surrounding temple complex were built during the reign of the fourth dynasty pharaoh Kafre around 2,600BC. This dating was based on three pieces of evidence. First, a stone tablet dating from the reign of Tuthmosis, found between the huge paws of the Sphinx, was inscribed with the first syllable of Kafre's name. This suggested he had some involvement with it but did not actually cite him as the builder. Secondly, statues of Kafre, including one in the form of a Sphinx, were found buried in the floor of the Sphinx temple. Here again, no inscription suggests that he was the builder and it was common for temples to be taken over by successive pharaohs.

Thirdly, known statutes of Kafre resemble the face of the Sphinx and since Egyptian sculptors from the third dynasty were adept at reproducing the faces of pharaohs, this was assumed to be some evidence that Kafre built the Sphinx.

Clearly Kafre's association with the Sphinx was that he repaired it or in some way altered it and he may in fact have separated the main body from the bedrock enlarging the passages between them, but he certainly did not build it.

Evidence of its much greater antiquity stems from the differential patterns of weathering and erosion, both on the surface of the Sphinx and the surface on the ground surrounding it. Both the great Sphinx and the fourth dynasty tombs next to it are carved out of identical rock. But on the body of the Sphinx and on the Sphinx ditch, there are eroded channels up to two feet deep, whereas the tombs are unweathered to the point where one can still clearly read the inscriptions carved into their sides. Consequently, the tombs are a lot more recent than the Sphinx. Seismic research carried out by one eminent geologist and confirmed by another has shown that below the surface the limestone which makes up the Sphinx was weathered to eight feet deep, whereas along the back the same limestone was weathered only to a depth of four feet. The only explanation for this overall weathering is water erosion.

The last substantial period of rainfall in Egypt was during the Nabtian-Pluvial when Egypt was subject to floods and heavy rainfall from 12,000BC to 3,000BC. It could have been weathered then, or alternatively, it could have been weathered during the breakup of the last ice age from 15,000 to 13,000BC and broadly speaking, I think that it's safe to assume that the Sphinx was built around the time of the end of the last ice age.

The ancient Egyptians themselves claim that their civilisation extended far back beyond dynastic times in recorded history and the Sumerian epics speak of a similar ancient tradition which leads to the view that since their pantheons of gods were almost identical (save for different names) both of these ancient cultures have a common origin.

Clearly as the ice receded, these ancient civilisations spread out across the globe creating the worldwide lattice of megaliths that I mentioned earlier.

Before moving on to deal with these ancient megaliths and their purpose to the first civilisation of man, I want to highlight two further pieces of literature which lend to proof of the existence of a very high civilisation in great antiquity.

The widespread belief in a golden age when men lived longer is common to all of the ancient advanced societies who share the common legend.

Quite by chance we now have a document which sheds some light on this question of longevity and that gives us an uninterrupted list of kings from the very beginning of the Sumerian monarchy down to the 18th century BC. This is the famous Sumerian king list compiled from about fifteen different texts and published in 1939. In spite of various imperfections, this document is invaluable. Not only does it embody and summarise very old Sumerian traditions, but it provides an excellent chronological framework in which we can place most of the great legends of the Sumerian heroic age.

The king list begins in the city of Eridu, one of the most ancient settlements in southern Iraq. It details a series of kings who rule for incredibly long periods of time and it has an eerie similarity to Adams posterity in the Judaeo-Christian Bible. It divides into kings of heaven and kings on earth both before and after the flood.

The Sumerian king list which describes individual reigns covering several thousand years also describes many of these individuals as gods. It's clear from this that the individuals in question were an extremely long lived nature whose lifespans on earth were further enhanced by their living or at least occupying from time to time the apex of pyramids.

When dealing with history, it's important to express dates in figures. However, unfortunately, in the ancient world there was no standard calendar, so at first sight it's a bit difficult to accept the Sumerian king list with its list of fantastic longevities. Nevertheless, there is some evidence of its accuracy!

In ancient times, the Greeks counted from the first Olympia of 776BC, the Romans counted from the foundation of Rome in 753BC; the Muslims count to this day from their hegira of 622AD and the Christian era dates from the time of Christ.

The ancient Sumerians in Mesopotamia had no fixed chronological system until late in their history when they adopted the Seleucid system from one of Alexander's generals. Before that time, they simply referred to the years of the rein of their rulers. Consequently, to express such dates in terms of Christian chronology would be impossible but for Claudius Ptolemeus (Ptolemy) who was a Greek astronomer and mathematician living in Alexandria. In the second century AD, Ptolemy included in one of his books a list of all the kings of Babylon and Persia from Nabonassar of 746BC to Alexander the Great, 336 to 323BC. This list is known as "Ptolemy's cannon".

Ptolemy's cannon gives the length of each reign but also the outstanding astronomical events that occurred during them, and it so happens that by putting together data from several Assyrian tablets, we can reconstruct a long and uninterrupted list covering the period between 911BC and 627BC. This list also gives the main astronomical phenomena of these times.

Therefore, between 747 and 631BC the Sumerian/Assyrian king list and the Ptolemy cannon coincide. To confirm this, so do the eclipses and movements of the stars that they mention. Further yet, astronomers have found that an eclipse of the sun which in the Sumerian/Assyrian list is said to have occurred in the month of Sivan (May to June) of their king's tenth year, actually took place on the 15th June, 763BC.

This is precisely the date arrived at by proceeding backwards and adding together on the list the years of each king's rein.

The absolute chronology of Sumer is therefore firmly established from 911BC onwards and is exact. There is good reason to presume therefore that the king list of Sumer is accurate as it refers to the earlier generations and if this is the case, it takes us back to a period almost 435,000 years ago during the Mindel ice age.

WHY OUR ANCESTORS BUILT MEGALITHIC STRUCTURES.

To move massive stones you have to want them placed elsewhere for a good specific purpose, otherwise there's no point in spending millions of man-hours on these projects. The purpose has to be profoundly important or there's no point in spending energy developing engineering techniques and mathematical techniques to move huge stones and to align these stones to exact and specific configurations.

No culture in human history has just "run up" massive stone buildings for the sake of something to do, and to understand why all the ancient civilisations had, as a priority, the construction of these vast buildings we must look to the developing understanding of low-frequency geopathic stress on the earth's surface.

In the first civilisation of man two symbols appear most frequently together, these are twin snakes spiralling up a staff which is then topped by a wind globe symbol. This has come to be used as a universal emblem for the healing professions in all the societies of man today. In ancient Egypt this symbol was revered as the staff of Thoth, a magical rod crowned with a sun disk and encircled by two rising serpents. It's come down to us subsequently as a potent symbol of the hermetic arts and as a representation of the mutual inter-reactions of the basic energies of existence.

In ancient pre-Christian Britain this was known as the Caduceus and the two serpents entwined around the staff were of opposite polarity in the same way as the yin and the yang of Taoist philosophy are of opposite polarity and the chi and sha living energies of Chinese feng-shui are of opposite polarity.

All of the great buildings and stone megaliths in the world are either aligned exactly with the north-south east-west axis of the planet or are placed in some exact relationship to planets and constellations. They're all aligned and placed with superb accuracy to such an extent that we would have some difficulty in replicating this today. Often made of huge blocks of stone which had to be transported many miles to the building site, they're usually jointed and set in place with a precision that speaks of an ability to work massive stone pieces with a high degree of accuracy and dexterity.

They occur throughout the world in a vast and intricate web of pyramids, temples, stone circles, standing stones, carved stones, giant seats, carvings on stones, spirals on stones, cups, cups with tails flowing down hill, snakes, dragons, hanging stones and pre-reformation churches.

They all occupy sites said to have been sacred to our ancestors. These sites often bear significant physical relationship to one another over long distances, sometimes forming straight lines which run for several hundred miles. These sites are "charged" insofar as they have a "feeling" about them which communicates itself to sensitive people who spend any time there and this is because they are all on ley lines. The flows of energy are best described by E. J. Eitel (1873) in his book on feng-shui entitled, "The Science of Sacred Landscape in Old China". Dr Eitel states "there are currents in the earth's crust, two different ones which, shall I say, are magnetic currents, the one male the other female, the one positive the other negative".

LEY LINES

Ley lines were discovered and named by Alfred Watkins, a Herefordshire businessman and pioneer photographer who spent years riding on horseback through the Bredwardine Hills. He observed the rural life which was, in those days, still ordered by the cycle of the seasons and the speed by which a horse drawn cart could travel along country lanes.

In the early 1920s, Watkins was looking out across the landscape and experienced a flash of insight where he saw spread out beneath him an astonishing network of lines linking all manner of ancient sites. Earth mounds and encampments, old stones, churches built on pre-Christian sites, Holy wells, moats and ponds and cross roads.

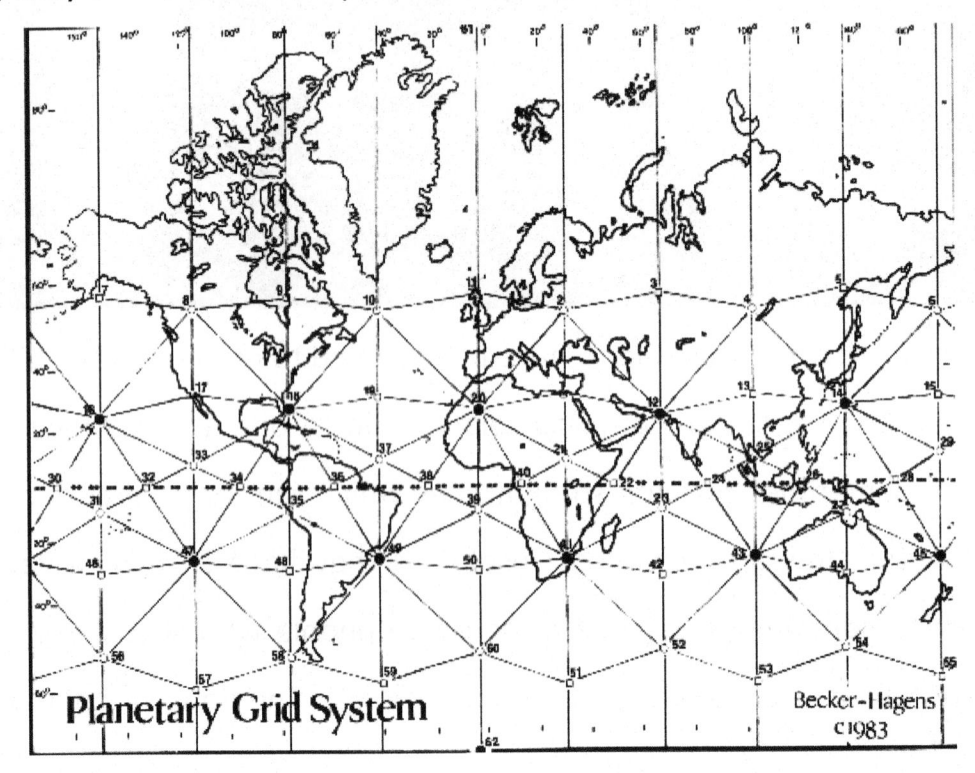

He saw this precise alignment as the remnants of a web of intersecting lines woven over the surface of the earth laid out by some prehistoric culture and preserved for thousands of years by the natural evolution of sacred sites. Delving into ancient literature, he found that certain names occur frequently on such alignments and believed that they were all linked by words denoting light. Amongst these were the words cole (Welsh coel, light or splendour) and ley meaning a clear glade relating to the Saxon leye, an early word for fire. This led him to call the lines leys and he spent the rest of his life exploring the phenomenon which he began to suspect was not simply the trade routes of pre-history, but concealed a deeper significance.

In modern English "to learn" means to "acquire knowledge". Further back in time the Old English version is "leornian", i.e. to get knowledge, to be cultivated. Further back the concept goes into the fricative thickets of Proto-Germanic to the word "liznojan" which has the sense of "to follow or to find a track" which stems from the Proto-Indo-European prefix "leis" meaning "track".

We know today that these ley lines are regions of the earth's surface where there are measurable anomalies within the earth's magnetic field.

The reason for these anomalies is that the very complex electromagnetic generator effect within the molten core of the earth sets up a very specific energy flow on the surface of the earth. This reacts with the incoming solar radiation to form a series of fixed eddies or lines of flow on the surface of the earth.

Ley lines can be measured against the dowsing reflex in most individuals, and represent an area with an induced voltage of 30 nanovolts around the region through which the magnetic field is changing. This is one millionth of the voltage necessary to trigger a nerve impulse in the human body, and can also be detected by measuring the fading of ultra short wave radio transmission in the 5 to 15 centimetre wave length on a commercial receiver.

Ley lines have two major components being made up of two streams of extremely low-frequency electromagnetic energy flow, having positive and negative charges respectfully. They vary in strength as the solar and lunar phase cycle progresses, and with a variety of other phase cycles of astronomical bodies. Ley lines were at one time entirely random energy flows across the surface of this planet but were later focused, guided and directed by the ancient civilisation so that they formed coherent structures which could then be used as a hard wired system of communication.

EFFECTS ON HUMAN BEHAVIOUR.

Recently, after collating data covering 2,400 years, the Russian scientist and doctor, Aleksandr Chizhevski has shown that all the world's major mass movement, including all wars, uprisings and social movements reveal regular cycles linked to sun-spot activity. The peak in popular unrest coincides in nearly every case, at or near the year of maximum solar activity and so mass excitability linked to each solar cycle can be divided into four phases. Minimum, increase, maximum and decline. These mark the progress of each solar cycle and this clearly shows that human behaviour is profoundly affected by the sun's "weather" and an understanding of this phenomenon by the people of the ancient high civilisation that went before us enabled them to control and manipulate these phenomenon so as to control their weather and to increase their natural longevity.

Solar weather = earth's weather.

The sun quivers like a giant jelly all the time and as it shakes and throbs it throws out vast quantities of charged particles in different proportions dependent on its degree of activity.

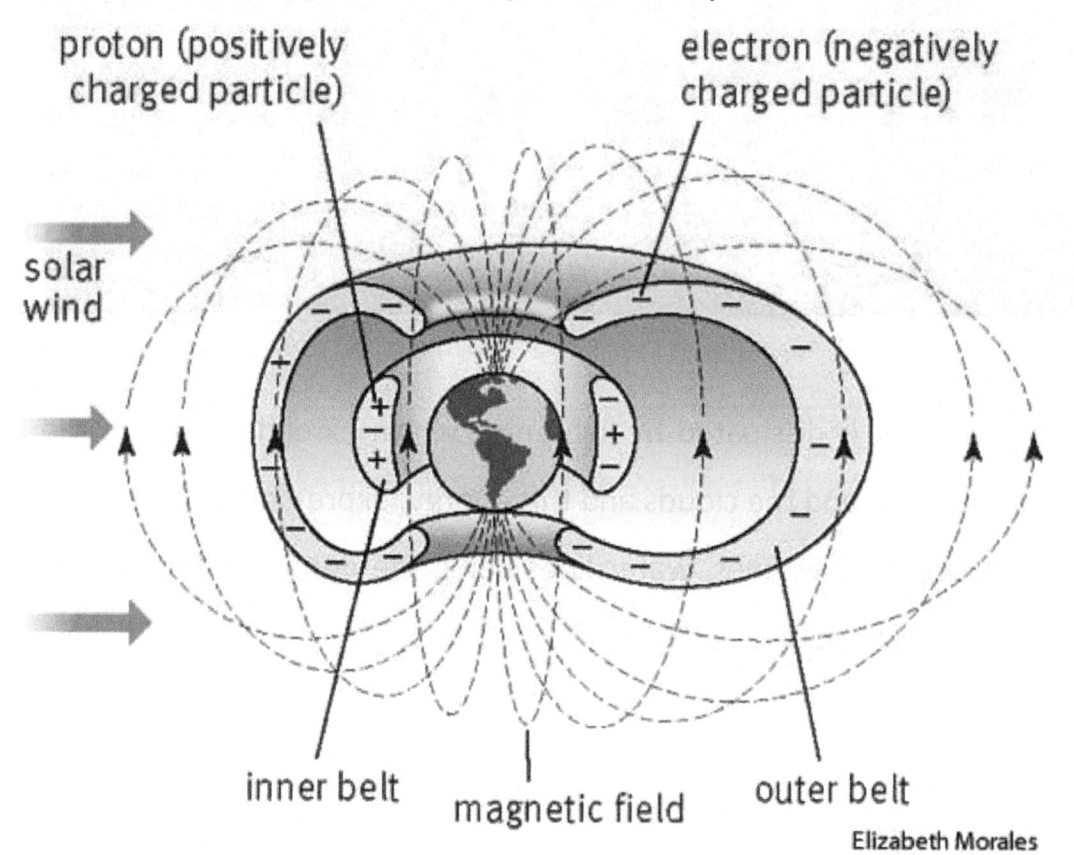

proton (positively charged particle)

electron (negatively charged particle)

solar wind

inner belt   magnetic field   outer belt

Elizabeth Morales

These charged particles impact on the Van Allen belts in the upper ionosphere and are deflected to the north and south poles of our planet where they can often be seen as the aurora borealis or the aurora australis.

As this energy builds up against the earth's shield, sprites occur and these are huge sheets of lightening which transit between the ionosphere and the upper cloud layers.

This energy in turn is dissipated by lightening which extends between the surface of the earth and the clouds and this energy, expressed as lightening, always runs along water lines, water lines being the dominant form of ley line along the surface of the earth.

This is all part and parcel of the electromagnetic energy structure of our planet and I'm laying it out here to indicate the close relationship that we have with the sun.

A clear understanding of this energy network and of the energy lines on the surface of the earth on which it impacts, led our ancestors to develop a technology which enabled them to collimate and use this vast store of renewable energy. For example, chemical reactions in the human body involving electron transport along metabolic pathways add up to a total current in the order of 200 amps. Since the energy gap of a protein is about 5 e V, this current represents an electrical power of about 1 kilowatt as being the body's maximum output. This is higher than the basal metabolic rate but is nevertheless a fairly accurate calculation. Therefore, a man with his arms up stretched approximates to a quarter wave dipole antenna at a frequency of 30 megahertz (10 metres wave length), the highest frequency which can reliably be reflected around the world by the ionosphere. This means that if a man could synchronize all of his chemical reactions to produce the energy of metabolism at a frequency of 30 megahertz, he would be able to communicate with a sensitive person anywhere in the world just using electromagnetic radiation. (On an Inverse-Square law basis for the propagation of electromagnetic radiation, the range for a transmitting power density of one kilowatt/metre squared could be received by a sensor capable of detecting 0.7pW/m2 at 3.7 times 10^7m which is almost twice that needed since the mean circumference of the earth is 4.0 times 10^7m).

This means that the dimensions of the world provide the limit for a single man-to-man communication but by using a group of adepts to transmit, perhaps holding hands to synchronise their respective power output, a more concentrated signal can be achieved, sufficient for coherent communication over long distances.

Sunlight at glancing incidence (which is sunset or sunrise), shining through the aurora of a group of humans, can be modulated by nonlinearities in the surrounding water vapour, so as to enable the sunlight to propagate a message ahead of the sun's rays in the manner of a forward scattering radar.

The concentration of festivals during dawn and sunset on the four solstices is common to all countries across the world, as is the concept of Holy sites. So the groups of trained adepts/priests at Holy or sacred sites (i.e. where a number of ley lines converge), could easily transmit and receive messages, visions, feelings or at least a binary code along these lines.

It can be demonstrated that the extremely low frequency electromagnetic forces running along ley lines can affect human activity and it can also be proved that concentrated human activity can affect the extremely low frequency electromagnetic forces flowing along ley lines.

Thus, it's relatively easy to envisage how a global Neolithic culture imbued with specific imperatives, i.e. to improve fertility of the land, to control the local weather system and to live to prodigious ages, can become a prosperous social system.

PUMPING POWER.

The ley lines are pumped by the interchange between the earth's geomagnetic field and the impact of incoming radiation from the cosmos on the magnetosphere as we've seen. They experience peaks and troughs in their activity which coincide with solar activity at the solstices. In the human population these mark the high and low tides of neuro-hormone activity giving rise to quite powerful, although subliminal, emotional tides, which result in enhanced excitability. These are often expressed as religious experiences or the need to dance and let off steam. Two of the most famous rites in Britain associated with the first solstice of the year are still performed in Cornwall, with the powerfully pagan Padstow's "obby, oss" and the more prim Helston "furry" dance, continuing a tradition that leads back to prehistoric times. These are good examples of the behavioural patterns reaching back into antiquity and during Neolithic times there was a global culture, one of the main drives of which was to map and adjust the flow of ley lines so that they could be used as a communication system, as a method of increasing fertility and as a method of prolonging life.

The placement of all the spirals cut into stone, the carved cups and tadpole shapes around the world, which are all sited on various energy lines are an indication as to the massive scope of this project.

A vast number of stones are set up with very precise alignments to deflect and realign the flows of energy into an interconnecting structure in such a way that this energy could be modulated as it passed through that structure. The placing of the stones (or earlier wooden structures) enhances the stability and sensitivity of ley line communication systems and serves as resonant antenna, amplifying the signals which flow along them. Different shapes have different properties, for example, the way that the pyramids focus extremely low frequency electromagnetic energy causes a gauss metre, placed at the centre of a non-magnetisable pyramid (in other words one made out of cardboard for example) to show a positive reading which increases in strength as the pyramid is brought into north-south alignment. Greater readings are produced with metal pyramids and instead of the magnetic materials of the frame shielding the interior of the pyramid from magnetic forces, the reverse is true because the pyramid shape itself focuses and enhances these forces.

In pursuit of fertility and local climate control, accumulators were constructed of alternating layers of organic and non-organic material. These were formed into hills, like Silbury Hill and indeed throughout the world, but particularly in Britain, 'toot hills' abound where energy is collimated to variously increase rainfall and organic (electromagnetic) activity. The expression 'toot hill' is an abbreviation of Thoth hill and relates directly back to the ancient high civilisation with its references to Thoth who in later Roman times became the god mercury. The two forces flowing up and down the Thoth staff are emblematic of the energies flowing down from the sun and up from the earth which come out of the surface as ley lines and can be concentrated using the organic accumulators known as 'toot hills'.

Earlier on, I mentioned that our ancestors were relatively more anaemic than we are by nature of the fact that they were dominantly vegetarian and did not come into contact very much with ferrous metals. This heightened sensitivity was very useful to them in mapping out their relationship with the energy flows in their environment but it made them more excitable. Indeed one of the main objects of the ancient rituals which still hung on until early Egyptian dynasties was the attempt, by the use of various rituals, to control and harness the energy of this excitability.

Chanting and dancing at particular locations at various times of the year were all part and parcel of this imperative and the civilisation which flowed from these understandings endured for many thousands of years in pre-history.

We can still see scattered remains of it today where the great Druid tradition lingered on long after the Roman conquests of the rest of Britain. In the west of Ireland, for example, there are stone towers often situated on islands which greatly enhance the fertility of the surrounding land. Similarly, across the breadth of England in southern Britain is the St. Michael and St. Mary alignment which is a broad band of energy some 20 paces wide running across southern Britain in an absolutely straight line bisecting the furthest western tip of Cornwall through Carn Gloos to the extreme eastern part of East Anglia. Recent computer calculations show that the placing of this line is very accurate indeed, and that it is perfectly straight, allowing for the curvature of the earth, over its entire length.

The St. Michael and St. Mary ley line is composed of two energy flows, positive and negative, which are directed through a series of sacred sites across the longest axis of southern Britain allowing for a flexing of up to 500 metres on either side of the line, no less than 63 churches fall within its boundary, of which ten are dedicated to St. Michael or St. George and 23 to St. Mary. St. Michael/St. George was synonymous with the sun god in ancient times and St. Mary with the earth goddess.

The image of St. Michael that comes down to the modern world is of immense antiquity. A Christian archangel is often shown thrusting his sword down the throat of a fearsome dragon and this supplanted older god such as Apollo or the Celtic sun god Bell.

With the coming of Christianity, all of the sanctuaries and sacred hills and high places were taken over by the Christian church which then proceeded to set up graphic images of St. Michael's sword piercing the dragon. This is an adaptation of the hermetic wand or caduceus where a central staff has serpents entwined around it in a double spiral.

St. Michael is also often depicted holding the scales of justice to weigh human souls after each incarnation before guiding them to the after world. This was one of the functions of the Egyptian deity Thoth, god of wisdom and scribe of the gods. The Ibis headed Thoth was the original owner of the serpent staff, Caduceus, and across southern Britain many natural and artificial mounds are known as 'toot hills' referred to, by some authorities, as having a special association with Thoth (or Tahuti) who was later overshadowed by his Greek equivalent Hermes, said to be the father of the hermetic arts and the originator of magic and religion.

Hermes had a special association with roads and standing stones, examples of which are called 'herm's' and were to be found at the centre of Greek market places. In Roman times the messenger of the gods was Mercury and they continued the tradition with Mercury stones marking Roman roads and so on into the Aztec pantheon where he is featured as the feathered serpent Quetzalcoatl, to the Gauls as Teutatis and the Muslims Idris.

The St. Michael line was constructed on an axis that aligns with the centre of our solar system at crucial times of the ancient calendar, and on Beltane, when our ancestors celebrated the return of Bell, the sun god, with his power to fertilise the land, the sunrise at dawn coincides with a line of sacred sites.

As the year progresses, the sun aligned to Llughnasad, the summer solstice, then to Samhain, the autumn solstice and finally to Imbolc, the winter solstice.

It was clearly very important for people to know of and be prepared for this specific sunlight and sunset festival four times a year since their agriculture depended on these cycles and to a certain extent so did their own fertility.

LONGEVITY.

The great pyramid at Giza is not a super tomb for a great pharaoh, it is in fact a huge power plant. It's the biggest building ever constructed by man, is about as high as a 48 storey office block and its base covers 14 acres. It's 450 feet high and contains 90 million cubic feet of stone, enough to build 30 empire state buildings or all the churches and chapels in England built since the time of Christ. It contains 2,500,000 stones ranging in weight from 2½ to 70 tons each and is the finest of the original 80 or so pyramids build in Egypt (30 of which still stand today). The stone for the construction of the great pyramid came from as far away as 500 miles and to this day very few people know how 70 ton stones can be placed so accurately or jointed so finely that you can't put a piece of paper in between them.

All of the pyramids in Sumer are aligned in such a way that each corner is orientated toward a cardinal point of the compass, so as to take advantage of the influence of the planets and constellations on earth radiation – "as above so below but in a different fashion". So they're all perfectly aligned, north, south, east, west. However, the great pyramid at Giza is aligned exactly to magnetic north and its dimensions are in perfect geometric symmetry in harmony with the golden number.

Nothing about it is accidental. Its position is the exact centre of the earth's land mass and the north-south axis is 31 degrees 9 minutes east of Greenwich i.e. the longest land meridian. The east-west axis is 29 degrees 58 minutes 51 seconds north and is the longest land parallel. Its weight is exactly 1,000 trillionth of the weight of the earth and enables us to calculate the distance of the earth from the sun which is 93 million miles.

WORLD WIDE WEB?

Many years ago when I was first practising Buddhism, I came across a story related by a German explorer concerning the use of Harmonic Power by Buddhist monks in a certain monastery.

"There had been a rock slide and an enormous boulder had blocked the mountainside path which the monks used cutting them off from the world. Beneath the mountain pass there was a flat plain and by scrambling down the rock face the monks were able to congregate on the flat plain where they formed into a semi-circle facing the mountainside where the rock was lodged. They then accumulated an array of the long horns/musical instruments that they use in Buddhist temples, also gongs, drums and groups of monks chanting."

"Placed in a semi-circle facing the rock face, they began to chant, drum and wind their instruments until they reached a certain pitch at which time the huge rock (which was at the focal point of their chanting semi-circle) began to shake and then rose from the path and floated down to the plain."

"Once it had reached its new location the monks stopped their 'music' and returned to their monastery to continue their practice."

A demonstration of harmonic power in action.

CORAL CASTLE.

One man who certainly replicated the feat of the Buddhist monks was Edward Leedskalnin, an eccentric Latvian, who immigrated to the United States where he laboured for 28 years to complete the amazing Coral Castle which consisted of a total of 1,100 tons of rock, some of which weighed as much as 30 tons individually. Leedskalnin stated quite clearly that he knew how the ancient Egyptians had built the great pyramid (and all the other pyramids) and took issue with modern science's understanding of nature. His concept of nature was simple:-

All matter consists of individual magnets and it is the movement of these magnets within materials and through space that produces measurable phenomenon – magnetism electricity and so on.

As we've seen, the earth, having properties of a large magnet, generates streams of magnetic energy that follow lines of force. Therefore, if we follow Leedskalnin's teachings that all objects consist of individual magnets, then it's safe to assume that an attraction or repulsion exists within all matter and that these forces can be harnessed to move great weights. So to overcome earth's gravitational pull, we need nothing more complicated than a means by which the alignment of magnetic elements within blocks of masonry can be adjusted to face the streams of individual magnets issuing from the earth.

If you think in terms of the forces used to lift a MAG-LEV train off the rail and where it can then attain huge speeds through lack of friction, then you get the idea of what Leedskalnin was talking about and also a good idea of how the Egyptians and other pyramid builders lifted the huge blocks of stone to build their pyramids.

Somehow or other a great civilisation of antiquity had found a way to line up all the magnetic forces within huge boulders in such a way as to enable these to lift off the ground under control. So the problem for them became not so much how to lift the things off the ground, but how to hold them down!

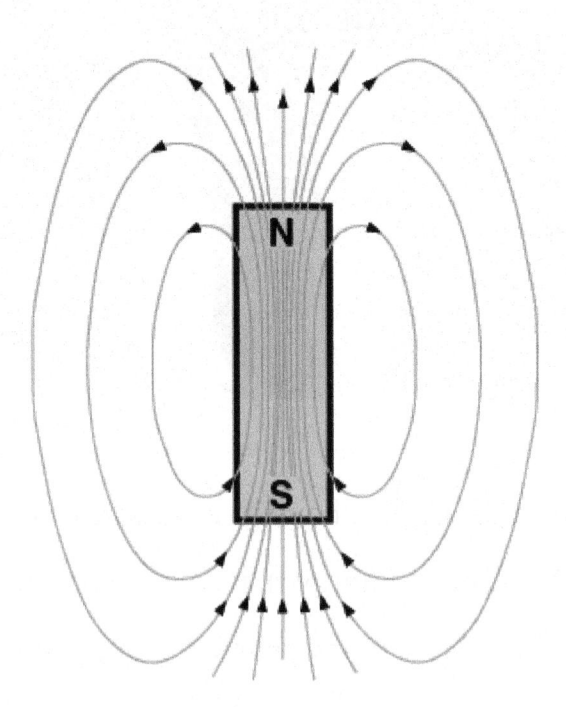

One way we use today to polarise the atoms in a bar of flat iron is to gently hammer it. Ultimately, this hammering aligns all of the tiny atomic magnets into a north south polarity in keeping with the polarity of the earth and in this way we create a soft iron magnet. Do this on a larger scale, for example, by wrapping a copper coil around a block and then placing another coil further out but around the same space, then by opposing the polarities of the currents flowing through the two coils, you can actually persuade the inner coil (and the rock that it's surrounding attached to), to lift off the ground. An easier way to do this is to vibrate the rock over a period of time until you hit the resonant pitch of that particular rock at which point, because it then takes on a specific polarity, will be repelled to a limited extent by the magnetic field of the earth and will lose some weight.

This is not anti-gravity in the accepted sense of there being some way of overcoming a mono-polar force like gravity but it is, for all intents and purposes, anti-gravity in effect.

Another person who understood this theory was Nikola Tesla, the physicist and inventor who developed the AC generator, three-phase power, the Tesla coil and several hundred other patents, all dealing with electricity and magnetism in one or another of their forms.

By applying a vibration machine (he called it an earthquake machine) at the resonant frequency of a building, he claimed that he could shake the building apart. He was reported as having said to the New York World Telegram in 1935, "I was experimenting with vibration. I had one of my machines going and I wanted to see if I could get it in tune with the vibration of the building. I put it up notch after notch. There was a peculiar cracking sound. I asked my assistants where did the sound come from. They did not know. I put the machine up a few more notches. There was a louder cracking sound. I knew I was approaching the vibration of the steel building. I pushed the machine a little higher. <u>Suddenly all the heavy machinery in the place was flying around.</u>"

"I grabbed a hammer and broke the machine. The building would have been about our ears in another few minutes.

Outside in the street there was pandemonium. The police and ambulances arrived. I told my assistants to say nothing. We told the police it must have been an earthquake. That's all they ever knew about it."

A reporter then asked Tesla what he would need to destroy the Empire State Building and he replied:-

"Five pounds of air pressure. If I attach the proper oscillating machine on a girder, that is all the force I would need, five pounds. Vibration will do anything. It would only be necessary to step up the vibration of the machine to fit the natural vibration of the building and the building would come crashing down. That's why soldiers break step crossing a bridge!"

If they didn't break step they could set up oscillations which would, and probably has in the past, destroy the bridge.

So now let's look at the worldwide web differently. The worldwide web I'm talking about is the worldwide web of energy lines, the flow of which was directed by the great civilisation and culminated in a plethora of pyramidal structures around the world. These structures (and particularly the great pyramid) were built to such dimensions as to enable them to become coupled oscillators with the earth and thereby draw limitless power from the earth's resonance.

In order for a coupled oscillator to begin to vibrate at the same frequency as the earth, there have to be two alternating timed pulses set in motion, one at the apex of the pyramid and one in a subterranean chamber located beneath the pyramid.

Once the vibration of the pyramid couples to the vibration of the earth, the transfer of energy from the earth to the pyramid can be sustained until the process is halted.

Power Out.

Once the pyramid begins to vibrate, driven by the energy of the seismic disturbances around the globe (and here I'm talking about an estimated 1 million earthquakes which occur annually) then power can be drawn from the pyramid. This power would come in part from the huge energy emanating from the earth and in part from the electromagnetic flow in the granite. The electromotive flow would occur when the quartz crystals in the rock of which the great pyramid is created are alternately pressed and released. Quartz crystals convert energy from one kind to another and in this instance would be converting pressure to electron flow.

This vast worldwide net of pyramidal generators fuelled the great ancient civilisation and all of the stone rings, megaliths and other ancient artefacts that litter the planet were part and parcel of this generation and distribution system.

All that is needed to extract enormous energy from the earth is to input the "grid signal" into the earth, and receive the enormous plate signal back. The standing S-wave is continuously replenished from the stress energy in the earth itself, as I've described above, so power may be extracted continuously.

To counter the earth's anisotropy, the pitch of the grid signal would have to be tuned frequently and this may account for the persistent legends of groups of priests, druids, adepts gathering together at significant points on the worldwide web to chant in order to keep the vibrations linked.

Flight paths and microwaves.

Clearly able to transport huge blocks of stone over great distances, it's clear from a variety of sources that the Druidic class in this ancient civilisation were clearly able to transport themselves along these earth meridians. That is to say, they were able to fly using the same technology that they used to lift and position the megaliths and in conclusion I quote from the brilliant Christopher Dunn's book, "The Giza Power Plant", ISBN 1-879181-50-9 (page 234).

"As evidenced by their ability to lift huge weights, both Edward Leedskalnin and the ancient Egyptians were utilising technology that we do not possess. Their ability to use gravity against itself and make large masses weightless forecasts the development of new technology which may include vehicles that use very little energy and that, conceivably, could break gently through the earth's atmosphere, however indefinitely at any point in space, and then safely return to earth. A society that is not bound by the effects of gravity is a society that is finally unchained from the primitive wheel (which Egyptologists know the Egyptians did not use) and the wasteful, albeit sophisticated, use of fire such as the jet engine."

Back in the 1930s, Antoine Bovis rediscovered the power of the pyramid shape to affect matter. He did this after finding that small animals that had lost their way in the great pyramid and starved to death had not decomposed. On his return to Paris, he built a pyramid to exactly the same proportions and found that he could use it to reproduce the mummification process. He then used this method for preserving fruit and vegetables but he was unsuccessful, at that time, in attracting any significant attention to his discoveries.

The first really practical application of pyramid power came in the late 1940s when a Czechoslovak radio technician patented a cardboard pyramid-shaped razor-blade sharpener. He was granted a Czechoslovak patent on this because one of the distinguished scientists on the patent board had used the razor-blade sharpener with astounding results. It took a further ten years of research by top metallurgists to find out how it worked and it was discovered that due to electromagnetic dehydration, which dried out the minute pockets of water which, when present, can reduce the strength of steel by up to 22%.

Following on from this, it was found that food placed under a pyramid improves in taste, coffee becomes less bitter, the taste of wine improves and the acidity of fruit juices are lowered. The energy focused by pyramids and flowing through pyramids greatly enhances plant growth and causes the rapid production of alpha and beta waves in the human brain with a higher than average amplitude.

Water placed within a pyramid undergoes changes in its electromagnetic configuration, and these changes bring it into a range of harmonious resonance with living structures, so that it develops mild curative properties. This harmonic power, in all its forms, is one of the main properties of pyramids. They very considerably slow down the ageing process, enabling individuals to live far longer by tuning their mental states to a higher level of resonance, thus slowing their metabolism.

They do this by harmonising the rhythms and vibrations which are present in all living structures (particularly alpha and theta waves). Smoothing them out and enhancing their amplitude so that they are effectively "tuned" to resonate more smoothly at their natural frequencies.

Pyramids concentrate and focus the extremely low frequency flow of electromagnetic energy passing along ley lines and across the planet surface, bringing it and focusing it into a range of resonances that are highly beneficial to life, being pitched at life's natural resonant frequencies.

The balance of focal resonance across a pyramid are red close to the base, passing up through orange, yellow, green, blue, indigo to violet and these focus resonances harmonise exactly with the proportions of resonance found in all living structures. This is why the Ziggurats were coloured in this fashion.

So if you imagine a ley line as being like a long thin stream of energy flowing through a series of well known points on earth, you can begin to see how the use of this energy became fundamental both in the healing process and in the process of becoming longer lived.

Here's why

Earth is pulsating with negatively charged free electrons in counter-balance to the positively charged free radicals which cause inflammation in the body. When an injury or infection takes place in the body, white blood cells and T-lymphocyte cells rush to the site and release a shower of powerful free radicals. This is called an oxidative burst and aids in the destruction of invading microorganisms and damaged tissue. Free radicals are positively charged molecules (short of one or more electrons) that search for free electrons to become stable. Normally, these free radicals obtain their missing electrons by stripping electrons away from pathogens and damaged tissue. This kills the infectious bugs and breaks down damaged cells for removal. As this remedial work winds down, excess free radicals produced during the immune response are neutralised by anti-oxidants or free electrons in the body. However, if the free electrons are not available, there can be prolonged chronic inflammation. This means a progressive shift in the type of activity going on at the site of the inflammation. You get the simultaneous destruction and healing of the tissue, but a harmful free radical attack on healthy surrounding tissue. As the free radicals continue attacking and oxidising healthy tissue, the immune system increases its response sending more white blood cells that produce more free radicals. Free radical activity is at the basis of chronic disease and the ageing process, particularly accelerated ageing and early death. Accordingly, in a society with an understanding of and an access to structures which connect the body to the earth enabling the conductive tissues of the body's meridians to become charged with "overdoses" of free electrons, then inflammation is rapidly overcome.

In this way our ancestors, members of the great ancient civilisation, were able to dramatically slow down the ageing process, become extremely healthy and remain so for many centuries.

This can be replicated using 21st century technology and it appears to be the one sure way to arrest the progress of degenerative disease and premature aging. However, that is beyond the remit of this work.

My concern throughout this part of this work has been to point up the existence of an ancient very high technology based upon an understanding of electromagnetics which we do not currently possess.

I do not here offer anything but a glimpse into the technical possibilities which this knowledge clearly delivered in the past and could well deliver again and I write this so that those "SEEKERS OF WISDOM AND TRUTH" who find sympathy with the thoughts that I expressed may go on to rediscover and reinstate this technology in order to save humanity from itself and build a far better, very different world in the future.

Satis.

HARMONIC POWER

PART VI

YONDER

YOUR LIFE AFTER
THE DEATH OF YOUR BODY

©Keith Foster, April 2013

YONDER

CONTENTS

Page Number

268	Your Life-force
274	Eternal Energy
280	Proof
283	The Binding Force
287	Acknowledgements

Section I - YOUR LIFEFORCE

<u>How creation works.</u>

Imagine every living and non-living structure to be made up of a complex of notes like a musical chord waiting to be played. And then see that as each chord or being vibrates in response to the current state of energy passing through the universe, eventually each one comes into being as a person or thing as it becomes a harmonic of the current energy field. As levels of energy in the universe fluctuate, then different types or kinds of chord are brought into being or go out of existence.

<u>Evoked potential.</u>

Everything that has ever existed and everything that will ever exist is there in the ether waiting to be (re)-created in the physical universe when the energy flow of time plays it.

<u>Resonance and damping.</u>

Everything in existence today is structured in accordance with its chord's complex pattern and its position on the scale of the universe is dictated by the energy level of its harmonic relationship to the current energy flow of time.

This thrust of energy into creation is damped by space into a form dictated by the interplay of the energy which flows in from the ether and the polarised cubic space lattice into which it flows.

The resultant holographic structure allows for each archetype to form in matter in its preordained form, which in the case of complex living structures is dictated by its DNA (antenna).

Like water flowing into a mould, energy flows into its archetypal pattern contained within the three-dimensions of space (and time).

How do you influence this process?

You alter the pitch!

Birth and death.

In the etheric state of being, your spirit vibrates at a very high frequency. This is because the ether is friction free (viscid) and therefore supports the eternal movement of energy.

When you are born your unique energy signature (spirit) enters into matter where it is slowed down by the drag imposed upon it in its new watery vortex.

Your body acts as an antenna collecting and collimating the flow of energy from the cosmos.

As you age your body accumulates toxins which reduce the efficiency of your antenna and ultimately your body ceases to function and dies.

Meantime, your energy has been shaped and altered by life's experiences. So when it re-enters the flow in the ether, it has changed to form a new you.

The level of vibration of the new you dictates the next resonant structure that you can occupy. So your rebirth is dictated by the way you have lived your life on earth.

The Life-Force

The energy which makes up all matter intrudes into the space time continuum only so far as to be contained by the countervailing pressure of space. Accordingly, life is maintained by its energy force only so long as it can resist the "pressure" of space into which it intrudes.

The purpose of this teaching is to enable you to understand and learn how to maintain your life force longer than would otherwise be the case.

This is not as complex as it sounds but embodies a series of steps by which the energy to which your antenna responds, is better received.

Quantum theory.

The Schrödinger wave function with the particle in a box model of quantum mechanics elegantly describes the harmonic structure of space.

This proposes a cosmos composed of coherent harmonic waves crystallising into matter inside a polarised cubic space lattice to form a fluctuating hologram or blue print in the fabric of space.

A new paradigm.

In all of humankind's history, we've perceived God as being an entity apart from ourselves. Someone or something that whilst responsible for all creation, somehow stands apart.

This kind of thinking has, in the last few thousand years, led human kind to feel separated from the rest of nature – a highly destructive short-term point of view.

The reality is that all life is "God". The energy that fires every living thing – the vital spark is God. We are all part of that great gestalt.

This way of looking at reality does not exclude anything since all things, from the smallest atom to the greatest galaxy, have life. Every living vibrating pulsating entity is part of the consciousness of God and we are all connected.

Energy.

Beside the reality of matter is the reality of energy, both of which are arranged in the ether which is the frictionless viscid eternal realm of movement.

When you go yonder from this life, you re-enter the ether altered in your energetic form by the experiences of this particular life, but still basically the you, that you will always be. Like waves on the ocean your energy rolls on ever changing, ever the same.

Everything in existence grows from a pre-existing pattern in the ether where it's waiting to form. Each and every aspect of life and matter and energy are formed and framed in harmonic frequencies around which patterns of matter can coalesce.

As life's energy flows through the scales of the universe, life forms come into existence and go out of existence in response to the fluctuations within the matrix of all creation. Each form plays a role in the whole, interacting with all to a greater or lesser degree.

I am a part of the consciousness of God and so are you, and so is everything. Fractals of a greater whole, we prosper in Harmony when the power of the whole flows naturally through us.

Wisdom accumulates in the timeless backwaters of experience, giving perspective to prejudice and allaying the pain of passage.

Energy is eternal. Once set in motion it cannot be destroyed but can only be changed into different forms. Your spirit is pure energy which animates matter (your body) for a time, before returning to its fundamental form.

This involves a slowing down and speeding up of your energy, this being dependent on the medium it inhabits at any time and these crests and troughs in eternity are subject to continual change and can be effected by a conscious effort of the will.

Section II – Eternal Energy

No matter how much you learn to live in harmony with the forces that form and surround you, you will ultimately die. People usually die because they clog up their antenna and make it sick so that it can no longer function efficiently and receive the variety of signals that combine to keep it alive. Otherwise people have accidents or meet violent deaths in war or otherwise and, in any event, everything alive must ultimately die.

When you die what happens is this:-

The life-force which spiralled into you at the time of your conception, spirals out of you again. Now, however, it is made up not only of the energy and structure it had when it came into you, but also of a vast range of influences and energies which have impacted upon it throughout your life. These forces include your memories without which you would not be you, your personality matrix which is formed throughout your life around the chakras or energy centres in your body and your mind.

Mind is separate from the brain and, whilst you are alive, your mind directs and controls your brain which, as we've seen, is simply a superb room-temperature superconductor. Whilst under the direction of your mind, your brain acts as a holographic computer capable of processing huge amounts of information. In fact, all the information that comes in from the rest of the universe all of the time.

Your body dies and goes back to the elements whence it came. However, your mind, spirit, eternal essence does not die. It simply changes in frequency to vibrate at a different level.

The Vortex.

When the spirit slows down into matter it leaves a clear footprint of its passage at the crown of your head. This vortex, which is the fundamental shape of all energy forms throughout the universe, experiences a drag as it enters into matter and this drag is the formative force in the accretion of matter in the first few weeks of your life when, as I've said before, babies grow beyond the amount of food that they intake.

All creatures (with the exception of man in his present state) live seven times the length of time it takes them to mature. During this time the life-force acts most strongly on them and they grow to physical maturity and up to a point where it is viable for them to breed, after which time, the life-force begins to slowly diminish.

When your body dies, the life-force leaves spiralling out of your rapidly degenerating body moving up to a higher / different level of vibration where it then inhabits a new body but not in the physical form as we understand it on this plane.

A higher state of vibration renders the new body invisible from this plane and communication between the two or more levels of vibration is very rare.

When your energy complex rejoins the vast ocean of energy extant throughout the universe it is, like a wave on the ocean, become part of what we call God - the universal consciousness.

Everything is made up of energy, of movement, of vibration. All vibrations are arranged in a series of octaves and whilst we peek at the universe through a tiny slot between infrared and ultraviolet, the electromagnetic spectrum proceeds to infinity on either side of these wavelength gate posts.

Heaven and Hell.

The theological concepts of heaven and hell have validity in this context, since our souls migrate either up or down the electromagnetic spectrum from our life standpoint and this direction is mediated by the way in which we've lived our lives.

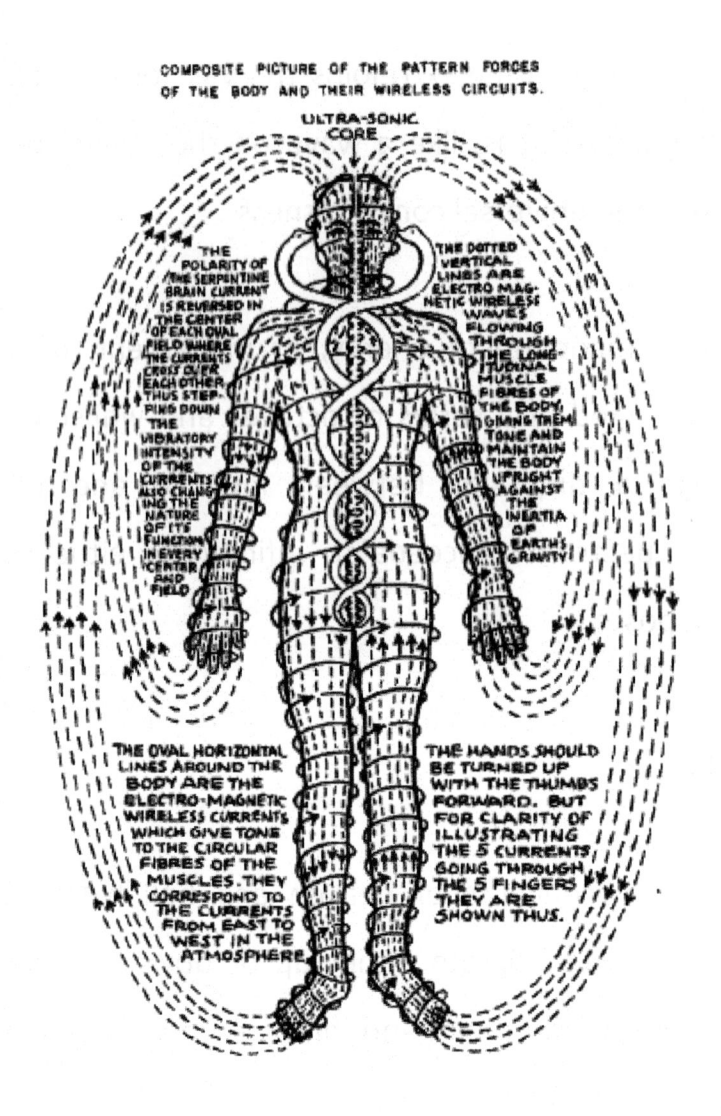

COMPOSITE PICTURE OF THE PATTERN FORCES OF THE BODY AND THEIR WIRELESS CIRCUITS.

ULTRA-SONIC CORE

THE POLARITY OF THE SERPENTINE BRAIN CURRENT IS REVERSED IN THE CENTER OF EACH OVAL FIELD WHERE THE CURRENTS CROSS OVER EACH OTHER THUS STEPPING DOWN THE VIBRATORY INTENSITY OF THE CURRENTS ALSO CHANGING THE NATURE OF ITS FUNCTION IN EVERY CENTER AND FIELD

THE DOTTED VERTICAL LINES ARE ELECTRO-MAGNETIC WIRELESS WAVES FLOWING THROUGH THE LONGITUDINAL MUSCLE FIBRES OF THE BODY GIVING THEM TONE AND MAINTAIN THE BODY UPRIGHT AGAINST THE INERTIA OF EARTH'S GRAVITY

THE OVAL HORIZONTAL LINES AROUND THE BODY ARE THE ELECTRO-MAGNETIC WIRELESS CURRENTS WHICH GIVE TONE TO THE CIRCULAR FIBRES OF THE MUSCLES. THEY CORRESPOND TO THE CURRENTS FROM EAST TO WEST IN THE ATMOSPHERE.

THE HANDS SHOULD BE TURNED UP WITH THE THUMBS FORWARD. BUT FOR CLARITY OF ILLUSTRATING THE 5 CURRENTS GOING THROUGH THE 5 FINGERS THEY ARE SHOWN THUS.

Looking at the energy centres in the body (the chakras) it's clear that we have a choice about where we want to base our emotional lives. Obviously, this emphasis on one particular dominant emotion or another can be changed by an act of will during the course of our lives. We are all made up of a cord of emotions, the emphasis of which note depends upon where we "live" within the matrix of our vibratory makeup.

For example, people who are dominated by very basic urges will resonate towards the lower chakras, whereas those who are of a different dominant temperament will primarily inhabit one of the other higher chakras.

That dominant makeup of your being will dictate whether or not you slow down or speed up when you leave this life.

Therefore, it's not a value judgment but a statement of the physical reality/the scientific reality of the leavening process which takes place at the point of death.

Great fear and sadness surrounds death, not because we're afraid of death, but because we're afraid of nothingness. The idea of being conscious throughout a great nothingness is insanity on steroids, but that is not the reason that I write this. I write this simply to point out that you move on when your body dies, you move on to new experiences, new realms of enlightenment and to a much greater understanding of all the vast complexity and richness that life has to offer.

You do see the people that you love again and you do see the people that you hate. However, love and hate become much more relative terms and since you are not embodied in the sense that we understand it in this life, you are much less open to pain and suffering experiencing instead a refining process with some mental but no physical suffering.

Dream state.

For the sake of clarity, what happens when you die is that you leave this dream and go into another one, a better one.

As of now, when you're sleeping you dream vividly and "really" since those dreams to you, at the time you're having them, are very real and very urgent. When you wake back to this reality, you are re-entering this dream and so it is when you die. You enter into another dream which is just as real, if less painful, than the one you experienced on this plane.

Section III - Proof

Neuro-physiological studies of the brain by Wilder Penfield and Nobel Prize winner, Sir John Eccles, have revealed that the mind is separate from the brain!

Both Penfield and Eccles use the most sophisticated laboratory instruments and the most rigorous techniques, over many years, to reach this conclusion. As Eccles told a distinguished scientific audience at the University of Utrecht, "the brain is only a useful instrument to serve the mind. This doesn't mean to underestimate the brain. The computer is a child's toy in comparison. The point is that the mind is superior to and entirely independent of the brain."

This is essential to know for the understanding of life since if consciousness is separate and the mind, wondering over the brain, gives it cognitive organisation and purpose, then we can clearly see that the mind is a concentrated energy field which has a life of its own.

Then, since the whole universe is energy, and energy is never destroyed, then the mind lives on after the death of the body in this phase of life, progressing through to a changed energy state of vibration in its next life.

All great religions subscribe to the idea of an after-life, partly through fear of death but more I think through the fear of becoming nothingness.

None of us can bear the idea of all of our experiences in this life being wasted and eradicated by death, so what I'm saying is that life goes on through many life times and the following is the proof I offer.

In his book *The Ghost of 29 Megacycles*, ISBN 0-586-06869-4, John Fuller details a series of experiments carried out by researchers, including Edison, Tesla and Marconi, attempting to contact people who have died and their energies gone yonder. Here I found persuasive evidence that life, after death of the body, migrates to a higher frequency on the Electromagnetic spectrum.

This evidence was rendered conclusive for me by a series of broadcasts made on Radio Luxembourg when I was a boy. Essentially, radio Luxembourg was commercial radio located 'off shore' from the U.K. licensing authority, so it could broadcast some pretty unusual content. Radio Luxembourg broadcast a series of programs in which listeners were able to call in and participate. Many contacts were made with the 'spirits' of long dead loved ones on these programmes, and much controversy took place between the representatives of established religious dogma and the people who participated in these programs. Under pressure from the establishment, the programs were taken off but almost everyone who participated gained a lot of satisfaction (and comfort) from being able to communicate, albeit in a limited way, with those who had gone yonder.

Let me be clear, the communication was not very precise as there were, and probably still are, technical and moral difficulties involved in such communications. However, the people involved were able to identify beyond any doubt those with whom they made contact.

Personally, I do not believe that people who have gone yonder want to be in communication with people at this level, and there may be very good reasons for this. But cite the above as yet another proof of life, on a different plane, after death – an example of the phenomena of 'ghostly electronic voices'.

Finally on the point of longevity, if you follow some of the advice in this work, you will probably increase the length and quality of your life on earth. But if you can go beyond that and live a good life in the sense of being a person who avoids inflicting pain of any kind on others and endeavours to lead a moral life, then you will improve your life to come. The choice is yours!

Section IV - THE BINDING FORCE

ZERO POINT ENERGY.

There are many worlds/levels of reality that we cannot see, smell, taste or touch. We know that they're there because of the existence in our reality of zero point energy. This is energy which comes into our reality and goes out and is beyond our ability to track or explain.

However, these other realities have one thing in common. They all exist on the electromagnetic scale. If they vibrate they cannot do otherwise and so we can conceptualise their existence, if not their substance.

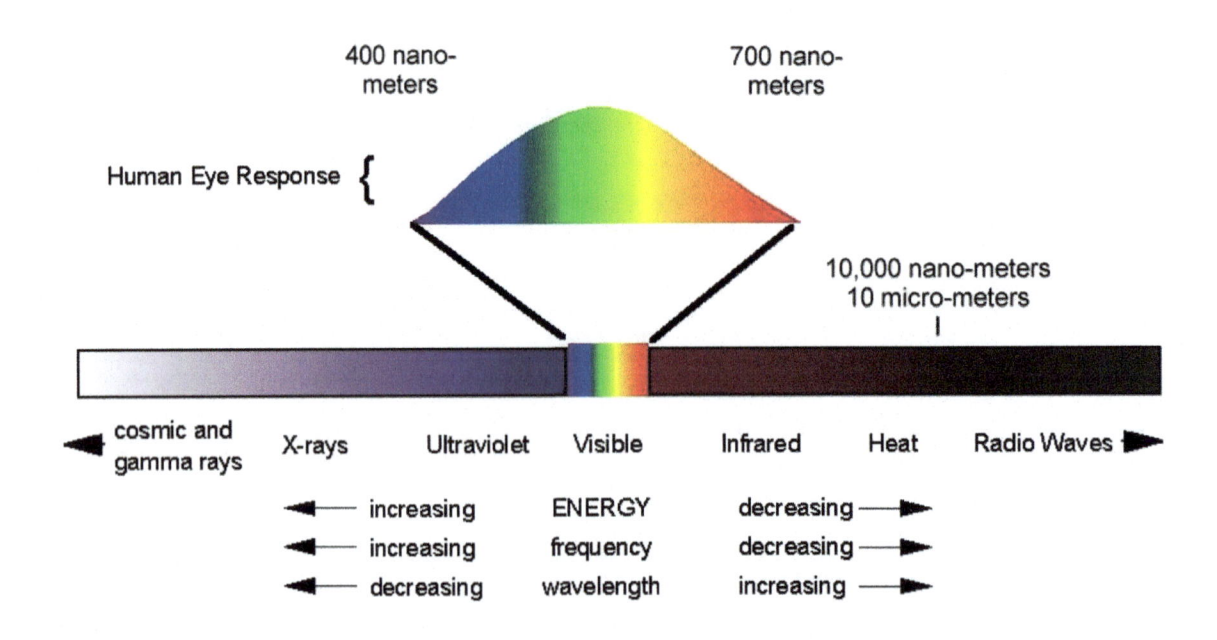

```
                    400 nano-              700 nano-
                     meters                 meters

    Human Eye Response {
                                                    10,000 nano-meters
                                                    10 micro-meters

    cosmic and    X-rays      Ultraviolet   Visible    Infrared    Heat    Radio Waves
    gamma rays

              ◄── increasing        ENERGY       decreasing ──►
              ◄── increasing        frequency    decreasing ──►
              ◄── decreasing        wavelength   increasing ──►
```

Space is not the empty vacuum of conventional theory but is in fact a seething mass of energy. Particles flash in and out of existence even in a vacuum chilled to absolute zero (minus 273.15C) which is the zero point of existence.

Billions of fluctuations occur every second and this forms the background radiation of the universe which you can hear as the static hiss on a transistor radio.

This zero point energy occurs on all frequencies and all wave lengths on the electromagnetic spectrum/scale. Therefore, at every point or every set or every octave of the electromagnetic scale there exist energies or states of being, peculiar or particular to that octave (connected by a zero point energy to all other octaves on the scale).

The binding force.

This plenum (the opposite of vacuum) flooded with zero point energy is the binding force of the universe. Within it lie all the energy forms which have their existence up or down the scales of the universe to infinity.

Your unique indestructible energy is a part of this plenum and migrates up or down the scale according to its "setting"/"tuning" at the point where it departs this life.

Information.

Just as is your body, your vital energy or spirit becomes a time capsule. It stores up all the history of your being from the distant past in ancient oceans, streams and forests where the environment shaped the basic anatomy of our limbs. To our colour vision and sense of smell moulded by life in ancient forests and plains. This is our genetic and energetic (as in vital energetic) inheritance as we graduate toward the light.

Although I have described our vital energy as a vortex reaching down (or up) into our physical world, I should explain that in fact this vortex extends well beyond the physical realm and is anchored, if anchored is the right word, in the energetic world beyond where it is the repository of the vast accumulation of knowledge and wisdom that has accreted to us during many thousands of life times.

We are all connected to the everlasting ocean of life throughout the universe and this connectedness is ably demonstrated in quantum mechanics where the action of one particle has a simultaneous effect on another particle at the farthest remove in the physical universe.

Finally, the best way of expressing this philosophy is by the use of a beautiful poem, the origins of which remain a mystery.

DO NOT STAND AT MY GRAVE AND WEEP.

Do not stand at my grave and weep;
I am not there. I do not sleep.
I am a thousand winds that blow.
I am the diamond glints on snow.
I am the sunlight on ripened grain.
I am the gentle autumn rain.
When you awaken in the morning's hush
I am the swift uplifting rush
Of quiet birds in circled flight.
I am the soft stars that shine at night.
Do not stand at my grave and cry;
I am not there. I did not die.

Bon voyage!

ACKNOWLEDGEMENTS

I am indebted to many great men and women who have gone before me in writing the various books and articles on which I base much of the thinking behind the theory laid out in this work.

I owe a debt of gratitude to the following authors from whose works I have borrowed liberally, in support of my own conclusions.

1. John Evans, **Mind, Body and Electromagnetism**, ISBN 1874498008.
2. Dr. Michael Colgan, **Your Personal Vitamin Profile**, ISBN 0856341401.
3. David Brownstein MD, **Iodine; Why you Need it, Why you Can't live Without it**, ISBN 978-0-9660882-3-6.
4. Jean Edmiston, **Inductance in Man**, ISBN 1857763769.
5. F. Batmanghelidj MD, **Your Body's Many Cries for Water**, ISBN 1899398058.
6. Jonathan V. Wright MD & Lane Leonard PhD, **Why Stomach Acid is Good for You,** ISBN 0-87131-931-4.
7. Clinton Ober, Stephen C. Sinatra MD & Martin Zucker, **Earthing – The Most Important Health Discovery Ever?**, ISBN 978-1-59120-283-7.
8. Margaret Hawkins, **Rebounding for Health**, ISBN 09520780-1-5.
9. Sang Wang, **Reverse Aging**, JSP Publishing, 888 S.W. 129th Terrace, Maiami, Florida 33176-5945, USA.
10. Gary Tunsky, **The Battle for Health is Over pH**, ISBN 0-9720636-1-7.
11. Dr. Robert Lustig, **Fat Chance – The Bitter Truth about Sugar**, ISBN 978-0-00-751412-0.
12. Paul Devereux, **Stone Age Sound Tracks**, ISBN 1-84333-019-9.
13. Keith Foster, **Perfume, Astrology & You**, ISBN, 0953240703.
14. Jeff T. Bowles, *The Miraculous Results of Extremely High Doses of Vitamin D3.* (e-book available at Amazon.com)

15. Christopher Dunn, *The Giza Power Plant –technologies of Ancient Egypt*, ISBN, 1-879181-50-9.
16. John G. Fuller, *The Ghost of 29 Megacycles*, ISBN 0-586-06869-4.
17. Max Toth & Greg Nielson, *Pyramid Power – Secret Energy of the Ancients Revealed,* ISBN 0-89281-106-4.
18. Keith Foster, *Lifelight – How to Protect Yourself from Cancer*, ISBN 09532407-1-1.

INDEX

PART II – GAIN	2 – 93
PART III – PROSPER	94 – 195
PART IV - HOW TO DRAW ENERGY FROM THE EARTH	196 – 213
PART V – THE GOLDEN AGE	214 – 265
PART VI – YONDER	266 – 286